PRAISE for
SETTING BOUNDARIES will s

"Get ready to learn a lot about yourself and unlearn the patterns that have kept you stressed, struggling, and resentful. I'm a big believer in setting clear, loving boundaries, and there's no better person to learn this from than Nancy. In her new book, *Setting Boundaries Will Set You Free*, she shows us that our boundaries are not only our responsibility, they're also the way we teach others how to treat us. Please read this book . . . and then give it to everyone you know!"

— **Gabrielle Bernstein**, #1 *New York Times* best-selling author of *Super Attractor* and international speaker

"Get out your highlighter because *Setting Boundaries Will Set You Free* is an incredibly insightful guide to freedom and you'll want to remember every word. Once again, Nancy has set the bar for using examples that really drive home the importance (and misunderstanding) when it comes to declaring and upholding boundaries. This should be required reading . . . for everyone!"

— **Kris Carr**, *New York Times* best-selling author of *Crazy Sexy Juice* and wellness activist

"I absolutely love this book and am buying it for my superwoman friends. It is an incredible read that will help you clearly work out where you end and everyone else begins. Reading it will help you reclaim your sovereignty, call back your energy, and create better relationships with others, but most of all yourself."

— **Rebecca Campbell**, best-selling author of *Light Is the New Black* and *Rise Sister Rise*

"This book belongs to you! If anyone asks to borrow it, say *no!* Advise them to buy their own copy. You hold in your hands a set of golden keys that will set you free."

— **Robert Holden**, best-selling author of *Finding Love Everywhere*

"Setting Boundaries Will Set You Free is the quintessential guide for empowerment, while presenting you with a profound opportunity for taking action with self-respect and self-worth."

— **Colette Baron-Reid**, best-selling author of *Uncharted*

"In this captivating book, Nancy shares heartfelt stories from her journey of being a classic doormat and people-pleasing superachiever. These traits eventually became the catalyst that inspired her to create powerful tools, which she shares in this book. Nancy shares how to create clear boundaries leading to improved relationships, greater vitality, and personal freedom. This powerful, must-read book is filled with practical wisdom and very useful tips."

— **Anita Moorjani**, *New York Times* best-selling author of *Dying to Be Me* and *What If This Is Heaven?*

"In her powerful, new book, Nancy Levin drives home the importance of making your needs a priority, highlighting how everyone in your life benefits when you do. She challenges you to claim the life you dream of and act to make it happen. With compelling examples and practical exercises, *Setting Boundaries Will Set You Free* delivers on its promise and leaves you feeling empowered and eager to draw a line in the sand with grace and love. A much-needed, go-to guide for creating the life you want!"

— **Kerri Richardson**, best-selling author of *What Your Clutter Is Trying to Tell You*

"Building and holding boundaries has been some of the greatest work in my life and career. Nancy's book supported me in up-leveling in a few profoundly important ways. With great boundaries come great success."

— **Alexandra Jamieson**, coach, best-selling author of *Women, Food, and Desire*, host of *Her Rules Radio*

"Nancy Levin is masterful at finding the core struggle within our belief system and shares practical ways to transform it toward clarity and freedom. Her heartfelt journey is a process of steps to identify where we gave our power away, understand the personal boundaries that have been crossed, take responsibility to guide ourselves forward, and envision a more empowered future. I love how Nancy helps us develop new relationships we may have with blame, self-denial, and guilt—to allow these emotions to be our teachers and create ways to shift them. The way Nancy leans into discomfort to guide us through is so inspiring! If you're ready to take the next step toward empowerment, this is it."

— **Paul Denniston**, founder of Grief Yoga

"Setting boundaries is the single most loving act I've done for myself as a writer. I could not have completed *Mary Magdalene Revealed* without fierce boundaries. Nancy Levin offers us the most critical tools to do the work we've come here to do, and to have the space for the lives we've dreamed of and the love we're meant for!"

— **Meggan Watterson**, *Wall Street Journal* best-selling author of *Mary Magdalene Revealed*

"By not setting boundaries, we abandon our true selves. With this book, Nancy helps you come home to yourself with her compassionate and practical wisdom."

— **Jessica Ortner**, *New York Times* best-selling author of *The Tapping Solution to Create Lasting Change*

"Nancy Levin is the perfect teacher and guide for this day and age. She's *been* there. She's lived it, breathed it, learned it, and now distills her wisdom in the kind of teaching that you can apply to your life *today*. This book will unlock parts of your life you didn't even know were locked, and will leave you with a gentle feeling of confidence that you are creating the life you want and deserve."

— **Nick Ortner**, *New York Times* best-selling author of *The Tapping Solution Manifesting Your Greatest Self*

"Nancy has written an incredible book that helps us understand the framework needed to have successful, fulfilling relationships. As a dear friend and as someone who has lead retreats with her, I have seen firsthand how her unique insights can help us make changes that bring us more happiness. I would recommend it as mandatory reading for anyone who interacts with another human being. My only issue with Nancy's new book on boundaries is that she took so long to write it. I wish I had read it when I was 20 years old!"

— **David Kessler**, author of *Finding Meaning, The Sixth Stage of Grief,* and co-author with Louise Hay of *You Can Heal Your Heart*

SETTING BOUNDARIES

will set

YOU FREE

ALSO BY NANCY LEVIN

Permission to Put Yourself First: Questions, Exercises, and
Advice to Transform All Your Relationships

Worthy: Boost Your Self-Worth to Grow Your Net Worth

Jump . . . And Your Life Will Appear:
An Inch-by-Inch Guide to Making a Major Change

Writing for My Life: Reclaiming the Lost Pieces of Me

All of the above are available at your local bookstore,
or may be ordered by visiting:

Hay House USA: www.hayhouse.com®
Hay House Australia: www.hayhouse.com.au
Hay House UK: www.hayhouse.co.uk
Hay House India: www.hayhouse.co.in

***

SETTING BOUNDARIES

will set

YOU FREE

The Ultimate Guide to Telling the Truth,
Creating Connection, and Finding Freedom

nancy levin

HAY HOUSE, INC.
Carlsbad, California • New York City
London • Sydney • New Delhi

Published in the United States by: Hay House, Inc.: www.hayhouse.com®
• **Published in Australia by:** Hay House Australia Pty. Ltd.: www.hayhouse
.com.au • **Published in the United Kingdom by:** Hay House UK, Ltd.: www
.hayhouse.co.uk • **Published in India by:** Hay House Publishers India: www
.hayhouse.co.in

Cover design: Julie Davison
Interior design: Bryn Starr Best

Library of Congress has cataloged the earlier edition as follows:

Names: Levin, Nancy, 1965- author.
Title: Setting boundaries will set you free : the ultimate guide to telling
   the truth, creating connection, and finding freedom / Nancy Levin.
Description: 1st edition. | Carlsbad, California : Hay House, Inc., 2020. |
Identifiers: LCCN 2019045277 (print) | LCCN 2019045278 (ebook) | ISBN
   9781401957551 (hardback) | ISBN 9781401957568 (ebook)
Subjects: LCSH: Boundaries (Psychology) | Assertiveness (Psychology) |
   Interpersonal relations.
Classification: LCC BF697 .L41253 2020 (print) | LCC BF697 (ebook) | DDC
   155.2--dc23
LC record available at https://lccn.loc.gov/2019045277
LC ebook record available at https://lccn.loc.gov/2019045278

Tradepaper ISBN: 978-1-4019-5757-5
E-book ISBN: 978-1-4019-5756-8
Audiobook ISBN: 978-1-4019-5758-2

12 11 10 9 8 7 6 5 4 3
1st edition, January 2020
2nd edition, January 2021

Printed in the United States of America

the anatomy of a boundary

the boundary is
the marker where
i can no longer be myself
no longer congruent with
or authentic to who i am

when i am about to lose myself
that's the boundary point

and yet
time and time again
we miss it

the disconnection from self
that amplifies
the way my attention pulls
toward you
as if my nervous system
is being dragged
by a magnet

i have been lost
and we are bound
i need to find
the rhythm
of who i am
without you
while with you still

the vital recalibration
back to me
knowing where i end
and you begin

my body and mind rest
restore and regulate best
when I am alone and
not satisfying
someone else's needs

slowing down now
i allow myself
the rest i have been
depriving myself of
by over-giving
and being on high alert

time to liberate me
instead of rescuing
everyone else
only i can restore
my resources

no longer willing to do
whatever it takes
when whatever it takes comes
at such a high cost to me

no longer allowing
an old commitment to people-pleasing
external validation and approval
to override my commitment
to my own truth and authenticity

the patterns we're running
won't dissolve by
someone else making a change

my boundary is mine to honor

we think our withholds
will keep us safe
but revealing
is what allows connection
and healing

CONTENTS

INTRODUCTION

As the Event Director at Hay House Publishing for over a decade, I was known as the person who could achieve the impossible. One particular feat illustrates what I mean. I was producing two back-to-back live events with best-selling author Dr. Wayne Dyer over a single weekend. He spoke in Atlanta on Saturday afternoon. Then, we flew to Detroit for a Sunday afternoon event.

Late Saturday evening, a panicked Wayne called me in my hotel room in Detroit. "I can't find my briefcase! I'm sure I left it somewhere en route from Atlanta." Everything he needed for his lecture was in that briefcase, and he was convinced he wouldn't be able to take the stage without it.

The overgiving superwoman that I was kicked into high gear. I remembered he had his briefcase in the van to the airport in Atlanta, so I called the car company. At first, they said they couldn't find it, but I begged them to check again. On the second look, they found it hiding under a seat—but it was almost midnight by then.

I called Wayne. "Go to bed, and don't worry. I'll figure out some way to get your briefcase to you in time."

I asked the car company to put an employee on a plane to Detroit, and they said they could not do that. My efforts to find a delivery service failed; after all, it was midnight on Saturday night.

I didn't sleep. At 4 A.M., I jumped into a taxi and used my laptop to buy the first available round-trip plane ticket to Atlanta. When I landed, I ran outside to meet the driver from the car company at baggage claim. Briefcase in hand,

I went back through security to catch the flight back to Detroit. TSA stopped me and questioned me profusely. Why was I was traveling with only a briefcase? Why was I flying straight back to the city I had just arrived from? I must have looked pretty suspicious. Who flies round trip just to pick up a briefcase?

Wayne was just waking up as I boarded the plane back to Detroit. I called him before we took off and told him I had his briefcase.

"Nancy, did you do something crazy?"

I managed to get to the event venue in Detroit just minutes before Wayne's car arrived. Ta-da! I could still claim my moniker of superwoman. I was so relieved.

Acts of heroism like this one were normal for me back then. Just another example of how I went to "crazy" lengths, as Wayne put it, to make sure I earned gold stars from everyone in my life. In the process—almost always—I paid no attention to what I needed for myself. I constantly allowed my own boundaries to be crossed . . . and crossed . . . and crossed again.

This was especially true in my marriage. But when you deny your own needs for so many years, eventually they simply refuse to be denied any longer. They end up getting expressed "sideways." For me, that expression was an affair—a sideways assertion of my needs in response to my constant refusal to set boundaries.

Making Room for the Real Me

It took eight years after the affair was over for the reckoning to happen—the one that would blow up my life. It arrived in the form of a voice mail from my husband as I sat in the San Diego airport, waiting for a plane to take me home to Colorado. "I read your journals. You'd better get your ass home—there's hell to pay."

I had a full 70 journals. Could he have possibly read "that one"? The one in which I wrote about the affair from eight years earlier?

The flight home was a blur. It felt like I was on my way to my execution.

When I got home, my husband was just inside the door, holding four of my journals. "I'm going to make copies of some of these pages and send them to everybody you know, including your parents and co-workers," he said. "I look forward to seeing what they think once they know the *real* you."

The real me. I had spent years hiding the real me. I worked hard to design a life that had *no room* for me. At that time, the idea that people could truly know me in all my vulnerabilities was nothing short of terror-inducing. I was sure, as my husband seemed to be saying, that I'd become an outcast as soon as they knew "the truth."

I was so afraid of anyone discovering my humanity that I was a champion "do-it-all doormat." I believed the only way I could be loved was by presenting my facade of superwoman to everyone in my life, from my family, to my friends, to my co-workers. I had to be the person everyone needed me to be—the chameleon who would put her own needs aside to make sure everyone else's needs were met. Who was I truly, and what did I need for myself? That question wasn't even on my map.

Not only did I fail to set boundaries, but I never even *dreamed* of setting them. Doing so would risk making someone else unhappy. To my mind, that was a risk I couldn't afford to take.

So after my husband threatened to tell everyone what he discovered in my journals, I still tried to make our marriage work. Ten months after that awful night, he kicked me out of the house. (The house I had bought and paid for, by the way.) Oh, and it was my birthday.

I returned and tried again. And again. And again. And again. The fifth time he threw me out was January 12, 2010, and that was when I finally put the do-it-all doormat on notice that she was no longer going to run my life. That fifth time, I finally asserted a boundary . . . by not going back.

That was the beginning of my quest to become a boundary badass. But it meant I had to stop saying yes to others' needs, wants, and desires in order to be loved and accepted. It meant I had to learn how to tell the truth and create connections with others in a more authentic way, rather than by wowing them with one selfless act after the next. It was a difficult transition, with lots of ups and downs. But I'm happy to report that the journey was well worth it. Following this path would lead to a kind of freedom I never knew existed—a freedom that has changed the course of my life forever.

What Is a Boundary?

A boundary is, in essence, where you end and another person begins. I define it as a limit that you set to define what you will and will not do, or what you will or will not accept or tolerate from others. (Throughout the book I will also use the word *limit* as a synonym for *boundary*.) Boundaries are completely natural and automatic. When the body hits its limit, we feel physical pain. When the heart or emotional system hits its limit, we feel anger, sadness, or hurt. These boundaries come preloaded into the human experience. Sometimes we can train ourselves to push past our natural limits—like the time I ran a 17-mile race over a 13,000-foot mountain pass . . . ouch! But there's no way to get rid of boundaries entirely.

So how do you know where your natural ones lie? You must be able to feel them, both physically and emotionally. When experiences feel decidedly positive, you're in the green zone. No boundaries nearby. When they feel neutral, or a little shaky—like you're not sure whether this is good or bad—you're in the yellow zone. A boundary is probably a few steps away. Then, of course, there are experiences that clearly feel bad. You experience pain—physical, mental, or emotional. When neutral experience gives way to negative experience, you know you're in the red zone, and a boundary has already been crossed.

Our emotional and physical systems are tracking our boundaries all the time. The trouble—the reason I'm writing this book at all—is that in many cases, our conscious mind is totally unaware we have a boundary, much less that it's been crossed. For lots of reasons that I will talk about in detail throughout the book, we have learned to suppress from our mind's awareness enormous amounts of information that are being registered at the level of the heart and gut—information about our limits and when they've been reached.

The result of this "boundary blindness" is that our natural boundaries are frequently getting crossed—and most of the time, we don't even know it's happening. Ever feel angry, resentful, shut down, or helpless? These are good warning signs that something is off. You've gone past your limit, and you're in the red zone. It's time to retrace your steps back to the place where you felt good, safe, and happy. The dividing line between positive and negative experience is a natural boundary that somehow got crossed.

Now you may be asking, "Doesn't negative experience *always* signal a boundary has been crossed? Isn't negative experience a part of life?" The answer to both questions is the same: yes. Negative experience signals a boundary has been crossed. And yes, negative experiences are part of being human. Having our limits exceeded from time to time in our lives is inevitable. We will lose people we love, get into fender benders, stub our toes and howl in pain. Nobody would choose *these* experiences, and often they are out of our control.

This doesn't mean we're powerless to create a life that is better and better with each day that passes, however. Too often I meet clients who have relinquished the boundaries over which they *do* have control, calling them inevitable when they are not.

That is what this book is about. Leaving the boundary-crossing acts of God to the side, we will be doing a deep dive with the ordinary, daily boundary crossings that we've been choosing to keep in place. The violations of our space, time, and physical and emotional comfort that we are allowing (consciously or unconsciously) every day.

So how do we set a boundary? We do it by naming the limits that already exist. We're not making up something new; we're just putting into words the needs and wants that have been there all along, under the surface. In this way, we make the unconscious conscious. We tell ourselves (and others) that certain experiences will not be tolerated, because they are not healthy for us and don't feel good. Locating and declaring our boundaries allows us to take care of our own needs—physical, emotional, energetic, mental, and material.

We all have many different types of boundaries. Here are some obvious ones:

Physical boundaries pertain to your body, your personal space, your time, and your privacy. For example, if someone touches you in a way that makes you feel uncomfortable, that person has crossed your physical boundary—even if it was unintentional.

Emotional boundaries pertain to your emotional needs—and the needs of others. For example, you might not want to stand by and watch while your mother berates your father.

Energetic boundaries pertain to the state of your vitality. Examples include picking up the energy of those around you, being overwhelmed by relationship drama, and regularly feeling drained during interactions with others.

Mental boundaries pertain to your thoughts, values, and opinions. An example might be listening to someone go on a misogynistic rant. You don't like what's being said—it feels terrible to you—and as such, your mental boundary is being crossed.

Material boundaries pertain to money and property that belong to you. For example, you may feel a contraction when your friends suggest splitting the dinner bill evenly, even though everyone else at the table shared a bottle of wine and you were not drinking.

Our boundaries are all about who we are and what *we* want and need. Boundaries help us feel our best and make it possible for us to live the life we most desire. If you want to experience more joy and excitement in your life, it all begins with boundaries.

The Benefits of Setting Boundaries

If you want a life of your own choice, if you want your own needs to be met more often than not, if you want the freedom to be your true self, and if you want better relationships, then you *must* learn to set boundaries.

Wait a minute. Did I just say that better relationships come from better boundaries? This is often the first objection I hear from clients. Turns out, most of us neglect to set boundaries in large part due to our fear that others won't love or accept us if we do. Won't the people in your life be angry at you for not acquiescing to their desires, and asserting your own instead? Well, some might—at least at first. But over time, if you're relating with people who truly love you and want you to be happy, your authentic needs will eventually be welcomed. If there's anything I've learned since my divorce, it's that relationships are much more genuine and intimate when we are completely honest with each other. There's less emotional discord when both parties are open about their needs. Staying in self-sacrifice mode is what blew up my marriage; it's simply not sustainable. Falsehood and masks are the enemies of intimacy.

We often presuppose that our needs and desires will be in competition with those of others. But what if every party in a relationship could have his or her needs met at the same time? In truth, our own desires aren't necessarily in opposition to what others want. Voicing them may even help others access their own true wants by example.

What I've learned is that if I'm suffering, my relationships suffer. My relationships have improved immeasurably since I did the boundary work I'm outlining in this book. I now prioritize self-love in a wholehearted way. I take *at least* as good care of myself as I take of the other people in my life. In fact, I've found that the more I love myself and take care of my own needs, the more love I have available for others. If I continually empty my cup trying to help others, I am left thirsty. It's like trying to squeeze blood from a stone. But when I fill up—by offering myself self-love and self-respect, in large part by honoring my own boundaries—my cup overflows. I have much more to give to those I love.

When I set healthy boundaries, I get my own needs and desires met more often than not. I then let everyone else in my life (including my significant other) be a grown-up and take responsibility for getting one's own needs and desires met. Bottom line? My needs are my job, and your needs are yours. Setting and keeping our own boundaries is an inside job.

How Do You Know If You Need to Set Boundaries?

Here are several "Boundary Needed!" scenarios I hear frequently from clients. Do any of these sound familiar?

- Your mother calls you five times a day and tells you everything you're doing wrong in your life;

- Your significant other leaves dirty clothes on the floor knowing you'll always pick them up;

- Your neighbor plays music very loud, disrupting your sleep;

- Your boss expects you to work overtime without prior notice or extra pay;

- Whenever you go out to eat with your friend, she tells you what you should and shouldn't eat;

- Your partner makes plans for the two of you without ever asking for your input;

- Your extended family members assume you will tell them every detail about your life;

- You're freezing in a restaurant, but you don't want to ask that the heat be turned up;

- Your aunt drops by your house anytime she wants, expecting you to stop what you're doing and spend time with her;

- Your teenager takes money from your wallet without asking, thinking you won't mind;

- Your partner consistently puts you down and acts as though you're overly sensitive if you feel hurt.

How many people's needs do you shoulder on a regular basis because you haven't set appropriate boundaries? For example, it's time to set some boundaries if . . .

- You frequently feel like a victim as a result of the behavior of others;

- You feel you have little privacy in your life;

- You usually let others make the plans when you spend time together, allowing them to choose the movie, the restaurant, or the vacation destination;

- You feel like you're a pushover when others express their desires;

- You prefer not to say anything when someone hurts you or cheats you (on purpose or accidentally);

- You feel it's virtuous when you put others ahead of yourself, and you feel mean and selfish when you try to assert your own desires;

- You often feel resentful toward others because they don't seem to take your needs into consideration;

- You're sure you could never set boundaries with certain people in your life;

- You've been able to set some clear boundaries in your life but want to graduate to true "badassery" in this area.

If you identify with any of the above, you probably believe some of the following common myths about boundaries:

- *Love requires that we set no boundaries.*

- *Setting boundaries will make me a selfish person.*

- *Setting boundaries will make everyone hate me.*

- *I can have the life I want without setting uncomfortable boundaries.*

- *I can't set a boundary because I don't know what to say without causing an argument.*

- *If I take care of my own needs all the time, no one else will get their needs met.*

- *If I spend my life setting boundaries, I'll no longer be a giving, generous person, and no one will want to be around me.*

- *Boundaries are restrictive, rather than freeing and expansive.*

- *Once I've set a boundary, I'm done and won't need to set it again.* (Wait until you hear what I have to say about this one!)

Do you hold to any of those myths? In this book, I'm going to bust every single one of them and reframe the whole conversation around setting limits. You'll learn practical strategies for locating and managing your boundaries with the care and attention they deserve. Only then will you be able to fully live the life that was meant for you.

Introducing Boundary Badassery

The way of living I've just described is what I've come to call "boundary badassery." It has taken a lot of work for me to become a "boundary badass," and it never ceases to be a learning process. But boundary badassery has completely changed my life for the better. It has brought me greater peace, ease, contentment, and well-being in every area of my life. When I ask for what I want and honor my own needs, I no longer feel guilt or a pull of obligation to take care of the other person at my own expense.

It's funny. The more I honor myself, the less I find myself engaged in conflicts about my boundaries. I have become more sensitive, so I feel pretty far in advance when I'm approaching a boundary! It's become second nature to name my limits—immediately—when I notice they're on the horizon. Plus, I do it without worrying others won't like me anymore. (Sound impossible? It's not, I promise. Just keep reading.)

If you've read my other books, you already know that everything I do is about self-love. That's because in my opinion, loving ourselves is the foundation of life—including loving others. When it comes to boundaries, loving ourselves means that we know we have a right to our boundaries, no matter what they are and no matter what anyone else wants. We'll compromise and negotiate when and where it makes sense to us, but we don't abandon the boundaries that are most important to us.

For those of us who have been the people pleasers, the rescuers, the fixers, and the savers, it feels radical to put ourselves in the position of priority, to check in with our own desires first, and to seek our own comfort first. I know it's frightening, and some of you may be shaking in your shoes at the thought of setting certain boundaries. Trust me—I understand. I've been there. But if a do-it-all doormat like me can become a boundary badass, so can you!

A Note on Inclusivity

The job of writing an inclusive book using the limited tool of the English language is a daunting one. Our language is itself biased and black or white, leaving little room for the beautiful diversity and ambiguity that make up our actual world. Moreover, I'm a white, cisgender, heterosexual, American woman—and there are going to be certain filters I bring to life and experience based on that identity.

Since the overwhelming majority of my clients happen to be heterosexual females, those are the stories that primarily populate this book. But I would argue the principles of boundary setting I'm teaching in this book would be useful for most people to understand and apply, regardless of gender or sexual orientation.

I've made the choice to allow the audience that has already found my work to speak for themselves on these pages because these are the authentic stories that have organically come out of this work so far. It's my sincere hope that their voices will touch your heart and your life, as they have mine.

About This Book

In the chapters that follow, I'll give you a 10-step process for learning how to set boundaries. I'll share more of my own story, and you'll read about many of my clients who have worked hard to set boundaries in all sorts of situations and relationships in their lives. Along the way, you'll do the same exercises I give my clients to discover what's standing in the way of your boundary badassery.

Here's the plan:

Step 1: Own That It's You Who's Been Crossing Your Boundaries. In this first step, you'll come to terms with a harsh truth—you're the one who has been crossing your boundaries all along. *No one else.* (Don't start fighting me on this one until you read what I have to say about it!)

Step 2: Take Your Boundary Inventory. Think you don't have any boundaries that need setting? Think again. First, you'll take an inventory of boundaries you easily hold and how you maintain them. Then, you'll take an inventory of boundaries that are overdue in your life. Both of these lists can be very eye-opening! Finally, you'll create what I call your "Boundary Pyramid," in which you'll categorize the boundaries you need to set by how important and difficult they are.

Step 3: Conquer Codependence. Many of us who struggle with boundaries are codependent. This means that we take responsibility for others to an extreme degree, denying our own wants and needs in hopes of meeting theirs. In this step, you'll learn that selfishness and guilt are actually not bad things at all.

Step 4. Excavate Your Unconscious Mind. It isn't enough to just decide you're going to set boundaries. If it were that easy, you'd have already done it. You must dig deep. The reason you don't set boundaries is complicated, and the answers lie in your unconscious mind. In this step, you'll excavate some of your unconscious material to bring to light what's holding you back.

Step 5: Get Comfortable with Short-Term Discomfort. To keep from setting boundaries, we tend to avoid short-term discomfort in favor of long-term resentment. It doesn't make sense, but we've all done it. In Step 5, you'll think about the discomforts you either avoid or take on. Then, you'll explore the fear of setting boundaries and create your "Dreaded List of Consequences"—the terrible things you're *sure* will happen if you set limits with certain people in your life.

Step 6: Envision Your Empowered Future. Before you actually start setting a lot of boundaries, you'll begin in this step to imagine what life will be like when you've mastered "boundary badassery."

Step 7: Write Your Scripts. This may be the most practical step in our boundary process. You'll actually write down what you're going to say when you set the boundaries you've chosen. Don't worry. I'll provide sample phrases to help you along! Then, you'll practice in the mirror and with a friend before you actually set your boundaries.

Step 8: Choose Your "Beginner" Boundaries. It's time to set some "beginner" boundaries that stretch you a bit, but not *too much* yet. I'll give you some clear guidelines for practicing with boundaries in this category. Then, you'll take a deep breath and have the necessary conversation to put the boundaries in place.

Step 9: Set Your Bottom-Line Boundary. This is the step where you *really* graduate and prepare to set a "bottom-line boundary," meaning one of your most important and most challenging limits. You'll start by setting it energetically through visualization and intention. You'll plan your script, revisit your "Dreaded List of Consequences," and create your "List of Exhilarating Outcomes" to remind yourself of what you'll gain from setting this boundary. Then, you'll set it!

Step 10: Repeat Until Free. In this last step, we'll talk about the reality of living a life of boundary badassery. The truth is that if you keep solid boundaries on a regular basis, you won't have to "set" them very often at all. We'll talk about the world of conscious choice, healthy selfishness, and how your boundaries will shift and grow over time.

This work was life changing for me, and if you're someone who has avoided boundaries for years, it can change your life too. Let's set the boundaries you need to create a more fulfilling life.

"Do I Need to Write Down the Exercises?"

The answer to this question is an emphatic *yes*! There will be quite a few exercises in each chapter, and it's important that you write down your answers. I'll ask you to refer to them at times, so you'll need to be able to find what you wrote.

You can record your answers on your computer or other device, or you can write them in a paper journal.

I encourage you to also write down any additional thoughts and feelings that come up for you as you read the book and complete the exercises. This is a journey of self-discovery, and if you take the time to reflect on what you write, you'll learn a lot about yourself. Often, when we go back and reread journals from a few days, weeks, or months ago, we gain important insights that can help us see and let go of limiting beliefs. Writing is a powerful process, so use it to your advantage as you engage with these pages.

My Invitation for You

I invite you to allow our exploration of boundaries to feel expansive and hopeful instead of constricting and fearful. While much will be said in this book about initiating boundaries to protect, preserve, or keep something out, your boundaries are also the way you can carefully choose and consciously curate what you want to bring in. Your willingness to feel the short-term discomfort of setting boundaries is the gateway to having everything you're longing for in your life. Truth, connection, and freedom become available to you when you make your preferences your priority, with courage and grace.

Remember, each time you set a healthy boundary, you're saying *Yes!* to you. I invite you to join my free Facebook group, Transform Together, at www.transform together.us to share your experiences as you move through this book. You'll get a lot of support from an engaged community as your process unfolds.

Let's dive in.

OWN THAT IT'S YOU WHO'S BEEN CROSSING YOUR BOUNDARIES

"I have said yes when I meant no," my client Valerie says. "I have had sex when I didn't want to. I have agreed to do things I didn't want to do. My mother constantly speaks to me and never asks for my opinions, wants, or needs. My ex-husband did the same. As if I was nonexistent. I've let people speak for me and make decisions for me. I've let other people control and manipulate me. I have been in situations where I wanted to leave but couldn't . . . until I became ill and understood if I didn't leave, I would die. Dissatisfaction, anger, and depression—I've experienced it all."

Valerie is not alone. Another client, Tina, tells me her story: "When I was amicably divorcing my husband years ago, I remet a man from childhood who lived in a different time zone from me. Texting turned to several long conversations a day. I was also working two jobs and heavily involved in my daughter's school. So I had little extra time available. I became sleep-deprived, short-tempered, and sick. When I set a boundary with this man to not text nearly so much, he became angry, blaming, and refused to accept my new 'rules,' as he called them. He insisted I must be lying to him and seeing someone. He needed to know my every move, literally down to when I showered and what I ate. I found myself explaining over and over what I was doing with my time. For a long time, I kept calling him back, even after his drunken rages, insulting and hurtful messages, followed by tearful apologies. I continued to try to appease him and calm his fears, even as I knew someone who truly loved me would honor my boundaries."

Here are some more stories from my clients:

Paula says, "My mom used to call me late at night. I asked her to stop calling me past 9 P.M. and ultimately decided to turn my phone ringer off after that time. There were times that I was still up at 9:00 and on the phone, and if she called, I answered. Then, I stayed up way too late listening to her." Inevitably, Paula would then become upset with her mother.

Faith was married for many years. Her husband didn't know she was unhappy about his drinking and that she wasn't sure if she loved him anymore. "I felt trapped and didn't think I had other choices. My husband didn't know what his drinking was doing to me, because I never told him."

Whenever Jessica's husband asks what she wants to do, she says, "I don't care," or "Whatever you want." "I sublimate my own wants because it seems easier," she says. In doing so, she treats her own desires and feelings as invalid.

Due to her upbringing in which her parents said no to almost everything, Zoe has found herself doing just the opposite, even when it might not be the best choice. As a result, she says yes to her daughter too often.

Valerie agreed to things she didn't want and stayed in situations when she wanted to leave. Tina allowed a man to abuse her verbally. Paula continued to speak to her mom late at night when she didn't want to. Faith never set a boundary with her husband regarding his drinking. Jessica sublimates her own desires for everyone else, and Zoe says yes when she wants to say no.

All of these situations point to a difficult truth about boundaries that is Step 1 of this process: *Own that it's YOU who is crossing your boundaries—no one else.*

Taking Responsibility for Our Lives

Yes, it's true. You're crossing your own boundaries in your life. Nobody can cross your boundary unless you allow it.

Ouch! This one hurts—I know.

But if you're going to learn how to set effective boundaries, you have to face it: It's your responsibility to recognize, set, and communicate the boundaries you need so that others have been given fair warning. Then, if your boundary gets crossed, you must take a stand and get out of the situation where your declared limits are not being respected. If you don't, you're crossing your *own* boundaries.

When it comes to the "everyday limits" this book is focused on, there simply is no such thing as someone else violating your boundaries. The responsibility is yours—not that of your overbearing parent, your annoying co-worker, or your unruly kids.

I didn't want to face this truth, either. For a long time, I felt my husband was violating my boundaries. His behavior was unacceptable, I thought. He should have been ashamed of himself.

But guess what? *I let it happen.* I went back over and over, expecting a different outcome from the same man. Of course, he *did* trample on my needs and desires, but only because I opened the door for him to do so.

Still not convinced? The next time you believe someone else is crossing your boundary, remind yourself that it isn't about that person's behavior. *It's about how you take care of yourself if the behavior continues.*

Most of us don't want to take responsibility for what happens to us, but the reality is that except in cases of violence (more on that in a moment), no one can cross our boundaries unless we allow it. If you believe someone else is doing something *to* you, you're stuck in a victim mind-set. If you're allowing someone to push through your boundary, that's a choice you've made.

It's much more comforting to maintain the victim mind-set that says our woes are the fault of others. But refusing to take responsibility for our lives and our boundaries means we relinquish what power and control we *do* have. We become resigned that our fate is inevitable; we fail to see that other choices are likely available to us. A victim mind-set causes us to see in tunnel vision, without hope for other opportunities and possibilities. Then, all we can do is complain and lament our fate.

But we're stuck in our circumstances only because we're stuck in our victim mind-set. The short-term payoff of staying the victim is that we get sympathy from others, which may offer us some temporary solace. But from a long-term perspective, we set ourselves up for a lifetime of suffering.

My client Tina has discovered how her victim mindset has kept her stuck. She hadn't named her boundaries around overgiving at home, choosing to let them be crossed again and again. In a nutshell, she needs time for herself—but doesn't take it, opting to instead cook, clean, and care for her family nonstop. Her current husband and daughter, on the other hand, have no problem taking the time they need for themselves.

"I'd get angry at my husband for playing on his computer for long periods of time or watching his TV shows in his man cave," she says. "I'd say that I wanted time to write and create, but I'd spend any free time I had cooking or doing laundry. My daughter and husband take all the time they need to recharge, and I've had a lot of judgment about it. I don't get recharged by playing games on my computer or watching TV, so it felt mindless and irresponsible to me.

"The biggest realization I've had from working on this boundary process is seeing how my husband has been mirroring to me exactly what I need to do for myself," she now says. "The truth is that *I'm* the one who's been irresponsible to myself by not carving out the time and space to do exactly what I need to show up more fully in my life. When I don't take responsibility for my own boundaries, I become angry, depleted, and resentful."

My client Gabrielle puts it this way: "Without setting boundaries, I'm looking for others to set them for me. I'm waiting for them to offer me the thing I want, rather than asking for it. When that doesn't happen, I feel disappointed and lost."

Of course, setting boundaries requires that we become comfortable with saying no. Ah, there's the rub! For many of us, the thought of saying no hasn't even been a *concept* throughout the course of our lives. My client Valerie is far from alone when she says she's spent most of her life feeling like she didn't have the right to say no to anyone or set limits on her time, money, space, or even her body. But when we don't say no to others, we're effectively saying yes to our boundaries getting crossed.

This inability to say no often extends beyond personal relationships into business. My friend Debra says, "I have a client who is well off financially but always tries to get me to discount my prices. She guilts me into dropping my price a lot, and I only do it because I think she'll take away her business." Debra has actually "discounted" herself because of her lack of self-worth. Yes, losing a paying client can feel dangerous when we need the funds. But as we come to believe in our worth, we gain trust and confidence. When a client relationship is no longer working, we can let go—knowing we'll soon find another client who's willing to pay our fee without complaint.

My client Elaine has come to the realization that she has only been able to set boundaries if she feels she's right and the other person is wrong. For example, if she believes her husband is wrong about spending their savings on a new car, she can set that boundary with him. But if she simply wants something like 30 minutes of alone time in the evenings, she struggles to set that boundary because she can't make anyone right or wrong in her mind in that scenario. Boundary setting isn't about "right" or "wrong," however. It's about what you want and need.

When we take responsibility for our lives, we empower ourselves to make decisions and take actions that fulfill our own desires. We take action to prevent our boundaries from being infringed, and that allows us to get unstuck from our undesirable circumstances.

You actually have far more power to create the life you want than you may realize. Moment by moment, you are choosing how you want your life to look and feel. When you choose to hold a boundary, you're choosing a life closer to what you want most. When you ignore your boundaries to keep the peace, you're choosing a life dictated by others' wants and needs. It's up to you to see to it that your choices serve your boundaries, rather than negate them.

Claiming this kind of choice is absolutely a game changer. Once you accept that you are responsible for your boundaries, you'll realize you do indeed have options in virtually every situation where you've previously felt trapped, suffocated, caught, or out of control. After all, *not* setting a boundary is also a choice!

Boundaries We Can't Control

I want to make it clear that the boundaries I'm talking about in this book are the ones over which we have some measure of control. I'm not talking about instances when someone has attacked you, sexually violated you, or held you against your will. The last thing I want is for those who are true victims to take on the responsibility for what happened to them. Far too often, rape and abuse victims blame themselves. This is damaging and simply untrue.

There are times when people can extricate themselves from violent situations by setting boundaries, but I'm well aware that there are other times when this isn't easy or safe.

Throughout this book, I'm talking about boundaries we choose to set or not with our friends, family, co-workers, and acquaintances. Even in those cases, however, I want to be clear that taking responsibility for the choices we make isn't the same as blaming ourselves. Nothing you read in this book should be an excuse for beating yourself up. Few of us were educated in how to uphold our boundaries, so you should not feel guilty or wrong for not having successfully upheld yours. If you begin to judge yourself, please stop and take a deep breath. Then, fill yourself with love to the best of your ability. Remember that I have struggled with many of the same boundary issues you may be facing; it's why I'm writing this book in the first place. We're all on a learning curve, so be patient with yourself.

Sometimes, however, life itself crosses our boundaries, and we choose to allow it consciously. For example, let's say you have a boundary against walking into a hospital because it evokes trauma from your past experiences in hospitals. But if your loved one ends up in the emergency room, you may decide you want to be there despite your boundary. Acknowledgment is the key; recognizing that you are making a choice to enter the hospital in spite of your boundary returns the power and responsibility to your hands.

I also want to take a moment to honor the ways in which systemic sexism and racism have made the playing field less even. Oppression is real, and it has a profound impact that limits choices for many people in numerous ways. Again, the exercises in this book are meant to help empower all of us in the small, everyday ways over which we *do* have control—which sets us up to help tackle the larger, systemic issues many among us still face.

That said, a victim mind-set helps no one, regardless of circumstances. Therefore, I encourage you to always look for possibilities that you may not have considered. Even when you think you have no choice in a situation, there's usually *some* amount of choice available to you. The choice might simply be mind-set—that is, choosing to take the high road when someone says something you feel is disrespectful, or opting to turn off the TV *just for today* because the news is causing you anxiety.

As Wayne Dyer said, "When we change the way we look at things, the things we look at change."

Why Most of Us Are Terrible Boundary Setters

My family was like most families in that boundaries weren't part of our vocabulary. Few of us are taught anything about boundaries, and the unspoken messages we receive about them are mixed. As a result, we don't know how to think about them, let alone create them.

Most families are so enmeshed that we often don't know where we end and our other family members begin. The result of this enmeshment is something I call "toxic empathy." We become so empathic with others—we learn how to feel what they are feeling so strongly—that we can't distinguish our own needs from the needs of our loved ones. If we become empathic enough, we may even lose our ability to determine where we end and *strangers* begin, trying to take care of people we don't even know.

For those of us in Western and many other cultures, this begins when we're children. As kids, we see that others—namely our parents and other authority figures—are allowed to set boundaries. Yet, in all but the most progressive families, a child's assertion of personal boundaries is unwelcome or even punished. There is good reason for this, as most little ones aren't the best judges of their own well-being. But it unwittingly teaches us to ignore our own desires, limitations, and needs.

We're taught to be good little boys and girls, first and foremost—to please others, always be polite, and do what we're told. We're even taught that self-sacrifice is virtuous. As a result, we may grow up feeling responsible for the happiness of others, believing that we have no right to say no to anyone else. We base our self-image on others' opinions, even allowing the people in our life to make decisions for us. Later, when we become parents ourselves, we might institute parental boundaries with our children, but we still don't know how to set boundaries with other adults.

It's human to feel that if someone else is unhappy or upset, it means we've done something wrong and we need to fix the situation. But often, we go to such extremes that we consider others' desires critically important, while our own are considered unimportant or even inconsequential. We skip over our own pain and anger—our signals that a boundary is nearby, or has already been crossed—and prioritize what the other wants instead. If we're uncomfortable with someone else's behavior, we believe we have to endure it; that there is no other option. We give everyone else the benefit of the doubt without ever offering *ourselves* that same benefit. We think it makes us "good people" if we take care of others, rather than ourselves.

We're told this selflessness is the recipe for a good life. So why doesn't it work? Why aren't more of us content and satisfied?

The Consequences of Not Setting Boundaries

When we're committed to people-pleasing, our lives are largely a lie. That was true for me for many years. I was constantly stressed out and always on high alert, fearing that I might be "found out." Someone might discover I

28

wasn't perfect, or I might fail to make sure someone else's needs were fulfilled.

I didn't know how to love myself in my humanness, so I lived a life of extremes. I paid no heed to my boundaries, which were largely unconscious and unknown to me. There was no way to sustain the pressure of how I was living, however, so something had to give. And it sure did give, with a vengeance—blowing up my whole life.

That's what can happen when we don't recognize and learn to set boundaries. Remember my story in the Introduction of flying round trip from Detroit to Atlanta to pick up Wayne Dyer's briefcase? If I'd had healthy boundaries, I would have told Wayne that there was no way to get his briefcase, and he would have had to do his presentation without it. Even though working without his notes might have been difficult for him, he would have survived. I mean, he was the great Wayne Dyer!

If I'd had healthy boundaries, I would have told my husband that I wouldn't tolerate him reading my journals, no matter what he found there. And I wouldn't have gone back to him repeatedly, knowing he'd treat me disrespectfully as he always did.

Actually, if I'd had healthy boundaries, there's a good chance I would never have had the affair that ended our marriage. If I'd asserted my boundaries with my husband all along, I might never have even *gotten* married. At the very least, I would have left the marriage rather than looking elsewhere for what was missing in our relationship.

When we go to extreme lengths to keep the peace, we compromise ourselves to the nth degree. We treat ourselves in a way we wouldn't dream of treating another person. And the truth is that no matter how much we try to please others, we aren't responsible for what they feel. Only they are responsible for their emotions, reactions, and needs.

By not setting boundaries, we abandon our true selves. The consequences are great—namely, squandering this precious life we've been given. We can't remain healthy for long, either emotionally or physically, when we sublimate our own desires for everyone else's—living for everyone but ourselves.

If you constantly feel put upon, as if your own feelings don't matter, the natural result is anger, resentment, and bitterness. You might succeed at suppressing this anger for years or even decades, but it's coming out one way or another. One day you might explode and shock everyone around you (including yourself!), or you may instead find yourself ill. There are countless stories of people developing chronic or serious illnesses, which they later recognize was caused by unprocessed, unspoken anger, rage, and sadness. These toxic storehouses are often, I believe, the result of poorly held boundaries.

You may not recognize your boundaries are being crossed until you find yourself in chaos. Not having been taught to notice and take seriously the warning signs in our own bodies and hearts, we aren't aware there's a problem until it's too late. It's the classic tale of the frog in the pot. When it's first put on the burner, the water is cool and comfortable. But as the water heats up gradually, the frog doesn't realize it's in trouble until it's already boiling. The same goes for you and your boundaries. You may convince yourself all is well, even as the temperature rises. But before you know it, you're cooked!

The "numb" phase can last years—sometimes an entire lifetime. We're so afraid of rocking the boat we don't look at what's really happening until it's too late.

One of the reasons we ignore our boundary needs is that we assume setting boundaries will cause conflict. We're terrified of discovering that others will be angry or disappointed in us. We fear that we'll end up abandoned and alone. So we sacrifice ourselves in order to maintain a false sense of harmony. But that isn't always the case. Of course, there are times when setting boundaries leads to conflict, especially if we're changing the rules with friends and family who have grown used to always being catered to. But often, our assumption that the other party will be upset proves to be 100 percent untrue. In fact, the other person may be stunned to discover that we weren't happy with the previous arrangement—and perfectly willing to make adjustments.

I know conflict is scary, especially for those who endured abuse, rage, or huge arguments in their childhood household. But not living a life of our own design is an enormous price to pay in order to avoid the discomfort that comes with setting boundaries.

Poet David Whyte once said that if we're living the life we truly want to live, someone we love will feel betrayed. That was true for my friend Rochelle. When she was 23 years old, she moved to another city, and her father felt betrayed that she was moving so far away from him. Twenty years later, he *still* felt betrayed. But she stayed in the city where she wanted to live, and her father had to accept it. If she had allowed him to infringe on her boundaries, she might never have had the wonderful life that her new city has afforded her.

Author Laurell K. Hamilton put it this way in her book *A Kiss of Shadows*: "There comes a point when you either embrace who and what you are, or condemn yourself to be miserable all your days. Other people will try to make you miserable; don't help them by doing the job yourself."

Here's a statement that may seem radical: Conflict isn't always a bad thing. It can simply be the illumination of our differences, and we can agree to disagree. No one has to be right, and no one has to win.

As I said in my book *Permission to Put Yourself First: Questions, Exercises, and Advice to Transform All Your Relationships* (formerly titled *The New Relationship Blueprint*), we have to learn to tolerate conflict. The boat needs to be rocked! We have to risk conflict in order to set boundaries and let our true selves see the light of day. We have to risk conflict in order to have the full life we were meant to live.

If you think this transition is impossible, let me be your example. After doing the work I outline in this book, I am truly an entirely different person. I'm no longer willing to package myself to be digestible to others and the world. I know that I'm as worthy of having my needs met as anyone else, even those I love the most. Abandoning myself for the sake of another is simply no longer a badge of honor—or even an option—for me. Even if someone is upset with me, it's preferable to self-abandonment.

And just in case you interpret boundary setting as callous and unloving, I want to be clear: naming my limits doesn't give me permission to walk all over anyone else's boundaries or refuse to be generous. In fact, I'm much more attuned to the boundaries of others now that I'm right with my own. And as for generosity, I'm now generous out of the desire to give rather than out of some fear that I won't be loved if I don't.

If there's one thing you need to understand, it's this: disappointing someone else isn't the end of the world. It's *fine*. It happens. And part of being a mature human adult is learning how to navigate it. I'm not suggesting you disregard common courtesy toward others; I'm only asking you to extend the same courtesy to yourself. Allowing yourself to be disappointed repeatedly, over the course of years, is a recipe for a miserable life.

You Can't Change Anyone Else

Here's another harsh truth about boundaries: not only do we have to take responsibility for our own lives and our own boundaries, even if someone else is disappointed, but we also can't expect anybody else to change in order for our boundaries to remain in place. In other words . . .

It's nobody else's job to maintain or respect your boundaries.

I know that's another *ouch*, but if you think about it, you know it's true.

Author and wellness advocate Kris Carr says, "The only time you can change someone is when they're in diapers." We might want someone to do something (or not do something), but it's that person's choice whether to do (or not do) as we ask. And it's *our* responsibility to ask—and then to make our next choice based on the response we receive. No matter what, our needs are our own to fill.

This may seem like a radical statement, especially when it comes to romantic relationships. We've been taught that our significant other is supposed to fill all of our needs. But that's an unrealistic (and actually impossible) romantic notion. We're doomed to constant dissatisfaction if we expect others to read our minds or take care of our needs.

No one else is responsible for our needs, and others' needs are not our responsibility. (Young children, of course, are an exception—their needs *are* a parent's responsibility.

That said, my clients have begun to set stronger boundaries with their children as well, to positive effect.)

My client Abby puts it this way: "I see it like touching a hot stove over and over until we learn the lesson. When I put responsibility on anyone else's shoulders for my needs, I lose. No one is going to do for me what I can't do for myself."

It's up to you to set expectations for what you will and won't tolerate and then make your own choices if your expectations aren't met. Other people simply aren't going to be as invested in your boundaries as you are. Why should they be? In fact, they may be invested in you "forgetting" or cowering from upholding your boundaries because they want to continue the behavior that encroaches on you (whether consciously or unconsciously). The bottom line is that your boundaries are *yours,* and they're no one else's responsibility.

This doesn't mean that you can never expect individuals to accommodate your boundary request. Again, it's their choice, just as it's your choice to stay in a relationship with them or not. For example, my former partner Aaron and I had very different feelings about unsolicited feedback. He loved to receive it and give it. I, on the other hand, detest unsolicited feedback. I don't want to give it or receive it because I feel criticized when someone offers feedback I haven't requested.

Aaron and I had to negotiate this with each other. He didn't want to feel required to bite his tongue, but my response to that was, "I hear that, *and* I'm not available for unsolicited feedback—period. If you insist on offering it, I will either leave or hang up the phone."

If he had consistently refused to honor my boundary in this respect, it would have been a deal breaker for our relationship. But his behavior was his choice, and my response to his behavior was my choice.

Zen and the Art of Boundary Maintenance

Suffering is caused by wanting something or someone else to be different from what is. So part of taking responsibility for our own boundaries is realizing that we can't count on anyone else changing to suit our needs. We have to look honestly at every situation as it is, and then choose the action that keeps our boundaries intact. This means we not only have to *set* each boundary, but we have to *continue to maintain it.*

This is a key part of the process that I find is missing in so many teachings about boundaries. Yet it's one of the biggest issues that my clients struggle with. They set a boundary and then complain, "But she just stomped all over my boundary again after I set it!"

The reality is that you can *count on* people pushing the boundaries you've already set. In some cases, even after you've set the boundary multiple times. It's up to you to draw a line in the sand over and over.

The fact that you can't change someone else means that even after you set your boundaries, you won't always get everything you want. Let's say you want your husband to stop gambling. But you can't change him, so you have to change the impact he's having on *you*. Here are some possible new choices you could make to uphold your boundary while recognizing that you can't change your husband's behavior:

- Let him know that you'll no longer put your paycheck into your joint bank account.

- Let him know that you won't give him money if there is any evidence he's still gambling.
- Ask him to move out, or go ahead and file for a divorce.

Tina and her current husband have created a list of "Things we need to keep our home happy." They've determined which responsibilities each will take on. Her husband agrees, but he doesn't always follow through. "I get tired of reminding and asking, and sometimes he's not here to do his part when certain things are needed," Tina says. "So I resentfully end up putting it on my list, and I do it. This is a constant practice and dance we do. I'm aware it's because I continually do what is his responsibility. He claims he forgets, and he quickly does them once he's reminded. But I don't want to remind him. I feel like his mother, not his wife, which annoys me."

Tina can't change or control her husband, so her choices include (1) continue to take on his responsibilities and feel resentful; (2) continue to remind him and feel resentful; (3) allow the chores to go undone, which might (emphasis on the *might*) cause her husband to remember his responsibilities; (4) leave the relationship, which she doesn't want to do; or (5) focus on the ways in which her husband enhances the relationship rather than what he doesn't do. It's up to her to decide which option to choose, as all of them are viable based on what she wants and needs for herself. The key is to make the decision from a place of conscious awareness.

One of the lessons Gabrielle learned as a child was that she was supposed to accept her family and others, always looking for the best in them. So whenever she tried to set a boundary, she didn't maintain it because she believed asserting her boundaries meant she wasn't accepting others as they were. But Tina's situation with her husband shows us that we have the choice to both assert our boundaries and accept others as they are. Again, we may not get everything we want, but we can often improve situations we dislike.

Here's what my client Renee experienced when she failed to maintain her boundaries: "My kids have come to translate my 'maybe' as a 'yes,' so it has become critical that there is no 'maybe.' There's 'yes,' and there's 'no.' And if it isn't a 'no' right away, it's 'we'll revisit this tomorrow.'" Since she hasn't been upholding her boundaries, Renee has essentially trained her kids to encroach upon them. It's up to her to reclaim her power position with her children by maintaining her boundaries as often as necessary.

When we don't reinforce our boundaries, we become like the child who cried wolf. We set a boundary but then let others step right over it. As a result, they don't believe we're serious about our boundary. That's what happened to Renee. After failing to maintain her boundary, she had to be even firmer about it. For this reason, I advise my clients to avoid setting a limit until they're ready to maintain it on a regular basis.

It may seem pointless to try setting a boundary if you can't change someone else's behavior, but I assure you it's far from pointless. In Step 7, I will provide tips for verbalizing your boundaries, but I want to give you basic guidelines now. That way, if you feel a burning desire to set a boundary before you get to the later chapter, you'll have an idea of how to do it.

The words we use to set a boundary are very important. A boundary is not a demand, like, "You can't talk to me that way!" It's also not an ultimatum, like, "If you don't stop talking to me that way, I'll leave you!"

A boundary is a statement of our needs and limits. We make it clear what *we* will do to take care of ourselves, rather than make a demand about the other person's behavior. The basic format is, "If you do X, I will take care of myself by doing Y." Here's an example: "When you speak to me that way, I feel disrespected. So the next time it happens, I'll take care of myself by leaving the room. Then, if necessary, I'll go to my sister's."

You've let the person know that you will leave because you've been emotionally triggered by the behavior. You don't have to fight it out or explain it further. You don't necessarily have to resolve your differences; you can have your differences and still stay in connection with each other.[1]

Let's say your partner becomes obnoxious when he or she has more than a couple of drinks. Here's what you might say: "I notice that I'm uncomfortable when you have more than two drinks. So if that happens, I'll find somewhere else to spend the night."

If your partner responds, "Fine! There's the door," it's still up to you to maintain the boundary you've set and actually spend the night elsewhere. Rather than hear the other person's statement as a threat, take an empowered stance and do what is necessary to take care of yourself.

What if your partner tries to convince you that you should stay? Simply remember this: It isn't okay for anyone else to tell you what's right for you. Only you are an expert on you.

When we set our boundaries in this way, we set the stage for no longer being impacted by the other person's behavior. We're no longer victims.

---

1   Obviously, if someone is abusive, I strongly suggest you remove yourself from the relationship permanently if you can.

When someone else continues to step on our boundaries after we've asked for what we want, it's easy to interpret that behavior as lack of caring. Often, however, it means nothing of the kind. It could be that the behavior is simply habitual or that it's the only thing the person knows how to do to feel safe. "I have the expectation that my husband will understand my needs because I tell him, but he forgets," says Tina. "I feel like I'm crystal clear, and yet, I feel like I'm living in a scenario like the movie *Groundhog Day* every day. So I have to accept his limitations as to what he can recall." She's learning not to make his behavior mean something in her mind that it doesn't truly mean. She realizes it isn't a reflection of how he feels about her.

Maintaining our boundaries with people we love is especially difficult. It requires that we stay connected to our own feelings so that we can tell where our loved one ends and we begin. To do this, we must take the attention off the other person and turn it toward ourselves. The other person's feelings are not our responsibility—but we often feel like they are. It can be a difficult transition to allow our partners to be adults who are responsible for their own actions, reactions, emotions, and choices.

This doesn't mean we become coldhearted or disrespectful, or that we never take others' wishes into account. It simply means that we stop infantilizing the people in our life. We take our own needs and desires into account *first and foremost.*

Most of us have spent so much time rationalizing, justifying, and bargaining with ourselves in order to avoid setting boundaries that we've abandoned ourselves in the process.

The Boundaries We'd Rather Not Set

Holding our boundaries may sometimes mean turning down an opportunity that we would love. Hay House author Robert Holden tells a story he calls "Saying No to Madagascar." He was invited to speak there, but he has a very strict boundary with himself that he will only be away from his children a certain number of nights per month. This particular opportunity in Madagascar, while utterly fabulous, would have crossed that boundary. So he made the choice to say no. Even if it's something we want, if it doesn't serve our vision for our life, it has to be a no.

Turning Blame into Self-Responsibility

Elaine had a situation with her oldest son (in his early 20s) that taught her an important lesson about the consequences of not naming her needs. Her family had gone to a boating marina, but her son said he didn't want to stay there with everyone. Instead, he went out on a boat, while Elaine stayed at the marina with her husband and youngest son. "An hour passed, and my son still hadn't returned," she says. "I had expected to spend time with him there, so by the minute, I got angrier and angrier. My husband kept telling me it wasn't a big deal. But by the time my son came back, I had worked myself into a rage and threw out a snarky comment about how long he'd been gone. That set the tone for the rest of the day. He shut down and put up a wall. I then isolated myself and found a reason to be mad at everyone, including my husband. I was in complete victim mode. The entire episode could have been avoided by 30 seconds of communication in which I asked my son to be back in a half hour."

"Around Christmas," says my client Laura, "I tend to feel a lot of anxiety because my husband's family always makes a big fuss. Even a seating chart for adults. It's so regimented, and they get upset if you fail to follow all of their arbitrary rules. So there's nothing pleasurable about spending the holidays with them; it's stressful and full of unnecessary conflict. But rather than set a boundary, I have always just blamed my husband for making me go there. He'd say, 'What else have we got going on?' I'd relent. We'd go. And I'd count the minutes until we left. A few years ago, I started insisting on taking two vehicles so that he could stay longer, and I could leave whenever I wanted. Last year, I told him I wasn't spending Christmas with them. I always felt justified in blaming my husband and his parents for making me feel obligated to spend time there. But I came to the realization that they can only manipulate me if I allow it. So what if they're disappointed? The boundary has never been theirs to maintain. It's my job."

Valerie has come to a similar realization. "I know now that no one has actually done anything to me," she says. "I have been a willing participant in every experience of my life. I still have to remind myself of this truth when I find myself wanting to blame someone or something for my experience. For the longest time, I saw myself as the victim of my ex-husband's behavior and endured his abusive outbursts. It took me a long time to realize that I didn't cause his anger, and I wasn't responsible for his feelings or actions. He was just being himself all this time. When he was angry, he wasn't doing it *to* me. He was unhappy with himself, and I couldn't fix that for him or change him. While I still struggle a lot with setting boundaries, I had to get out of that relationship in order to survive. I know now that my only responsibility is to take care of myself and not stay a victim. I always have a choice."

"I don't speak up about what I want in my relationships," my client Sharon says. "I sacrifice what I want so the other person is happy. Eventually, I feel resentful and assume the other person doesn't care about my needs. Then, I blame my partner for my needs not being met. I see now that when I begin to feel resentful, passive aggressive, or angry, it's a sign that I didn't set a boundary. I told myself that my ex-fiancé was an asshole. I said he stole my peace, joy, and lots of my money. In fact, I let him into my life, let him cross my boundaries, and willingly gave him money. He didn't force me to do any of these things. But for a long time, I blamed him. My life truly began when I reframed it to the truth, taking responsibility for allowing him to cross my boundaries. I learned what it meant to own my part in what happened, accept it, let go, and move on."

"I used to blame my former boss for keeping me late at work," my client Brenda says. "I didn't see it was my own responsibility to set and maintain a boundary. I was worried about losing my job or creating conflict that would make my work atmosphere tense. I felt out of control in the situation. It wasn't until after I left that job that I could see how I was to blame for my inability to stand up for what was best for me." After that, Brenda told recruiters that she didn't want a job with long hours.

Similarly, Gabrielle used to tell herself that she couldn't afford to change jobs even though she was miserable. But if she doesn't make an effort to find a better job, it's still a choice she's making.

When we finally turn our victim stories around and take responsibility for our boundaries, we become empowered in a new way. We see that there are choices available to us that we may not have seen before. Then, it's up to us to make those choices.

I know very well how difficult it can be to stop blaming the person or people you're certain are responsible for your circumstances. But challenge yourself to see the choices you've made that have contributed to the situation. Then, envision the different choices you could make instead.

Here's another harsh truth: Even though it's your responsibility to set a boundary, you may very well be in a difficult situation. You might legitimately be faced with the decision between allowing your boundaries to be crossed and ending an important relationship. Let's say your partner refuses to discipline your children, so you're the one who always has to set limits with your kids. Is he to blame for this? What choices do you have? You could ask your partner to sit down and have a conversation about discipline. If you fail to come to an agreement, you could ask him to see a therapist with you. If things don't improve, then you have the choice to live with the difference—or choose to leave the marriage.

There is nothing easy about this decision. As I said earlier in the chapter, since you can't change others, there will be times when you won't get everything you want. You can only do your best to create situations in which your boundaries are not infringed. While you may not be able to make it perfect, you'll certainly have a much better chance of designing the life you want if you know your boundaries and are willing to communicate and stand up for them.

Let's take a look at the boundaries you'd like to set in your life from this new perspective of responsibility and choice.

REMEMBER

It's *you* who has been
crossing your boundaries,
and it's your responsibility
to maintain your boundaries
as often as necessary,
or leave situations in
which your boundaries
are infringed.

TAKE YOUR
BOUNDARY INVENTORY

"I'll never forget exactly where I was and how I felt when I realized that I rarely had any independent thoughts," my client Gabrielle says. "I was seven years out of my Ph.D. and had been hired as a national consultant. While at a conference, I was talking to others in the group and heard myself say, 'My husband says . . .' and 'My husband thinks . . .' Those words stunned me because I realized that I wasn't articulating any of my own opinions. I didn't think they were worthy of being spoken."

Due to her upbringing, Gabrielle grew up believing if someone crossed one of her boundaries, it was unfortunate but something she had to accept. Love, in her world, meant never setting a boundary.

"When I think about setting a boundary, at first I feel brave," she says. "Then, I feel like I'm a bad person for not being more accommodating. I feel physically shaken and ill. Setting a boundary feels like a mean thing to do." At some point, she started avoiding certain people so that she didn't have to face setting boundaries—or live with the consequences of not setting them.

For my client Yvonne, staying in her emotionally abusive relationship for so long ultimately cost her everything. She was forced out of her home, and she lost her car and belongings. After 14 years of enduring the abuse, she lost control and struck her husband. He then filed charges.

Tina knew the parking lot at her office was unsafe with severe potholes and uneven pavement. She told her superiors about it, both verbally and in writing, with suggestions for making it safer, but they did nothing about it. The boundary she needed to set was to say she would leave the job if it wasn't fixed, but out of fear of being unemployed she stayed in the job. Eventually, she fell in the lot—twice. The last fall resulted in a back fracture that permanently damaged both of her knees and forced her to leave the job anyway in order to heal.

Elaine recalls an incident years ago when she got in the car with a friend who was drunk even though every alarm bell was going off inside of her. "I didn't know how to stick up for myself without appearing 'crazy' or 'too conservative.'" At that time in her life, she cared more about what other people thought than she cared about her own safety.

Much like me, boundaries weren't a familiar concept for Gabrielle, Yvonne, Tina, or Elaine. Through doing the work outlined in this book, they have realized they've allowed their boundaries to be violated in ways they never recognized before. While they were all raised differently, none was taught how to set and hold a boundary. These women grew up assuming it was "normal" to go with the flow and keep the peace, even when it felt terrible.

For many of us, taking proper care of ourselves by setting healthy boundaries requires conscious effort. It's actually natural to tend to our own needs and desires, but we've been taught to *unnaturally* put these needs and desires aside. So we deprive ourselves of our own comfort, in order to make others comfortable.

Obviously, my clients have suffered enormous consequences from avoiding boundaries, and it's clear that not setting boundaries is largely a result of lack of self-love. I've said it in previous books, and I'll say it again: Everything I teach is about self-love. This includes learning to set and hold our boundaries. This is why it's so important to begin to ask ourselves, "Am I taking care of myself by setting limits that feel good to *me*? What boundaries should I be setting that I'm avoiding?"

These questions are an exercise in aha moments for most of us. If what we want in life is more enjoyment, inner peace, satisfaction, and authentic connection, we have to wake up to the places where we are currently tolerating the opposite. That's why Step 2 on the journey is *Take Your Boundary Inventory.* Think of it as writing your personal boundary to-do list—all the places you really need to start saying no in your life.

The Origins and Consequences of Self-Sacrifice

Most cultures around the world have historically revered martyrdom. We're taught that self-sacrifice is a virtue; that the more we take care of others, the better. From the time we're little kids we get the message—in school and often at home—that we aren't worthy of love unless we're good. What does *goodness* mean? Keeping others happy, even if it means sacrificing our own happiness in the process.

But this is flawed, unhealthy thinking—and it's time our cultural norm got an upgrade. Studies are starting to correlate self-sacrifice with depression and high stress.

A 2017 study published in the journal *Nature Human Behaviour,* for example, showed that nicer, more sensitive people are more likely to be depressed than those who are more selfish.

When we don't take care of ourselves, our health, well-being, and relationships all suffer. When we are trained in overgiving, we tend to draw "over-takers" into our lives. After all, if you need to be selflessly taking care of others in order to feel safe, you'll need to find others who are willing to receive your devoted care! But of course, this kind of relationship is not equal, balanced, or—let me just say this from experience—fun! As I mentioned in the last chapter, it can be easy to point fingers at others, accusing them in our own minds of taking, taking, taking. But this road runs two ways. If you weren't willing to give, give, give, the dance would be over.

Unconsciously, we believe the consequences of being seen as a bad person—or worse yet, *selfish*—are that we'll be ostracized, abandoned, unloved, and alone. Rather than face such a horrible fate, we twist ourselves into all sorts of knots to appear acceptable to others. This tendency becomes particularly pronounced in our teen years when being accepted by our peers feels like an absolute necessity. We deny who we truly are and conform to what our social group considers cool. We do things we don't really want to do and allow others to treat us in ways that are hurtful—all in the name of being accepted. We go with the flow even if it means we feel disrespected, infringed upon, and abused.

Another origin of this behavior is the unconscious belief that we don't deserve to be treated respectfully. We see others as more worthy than we are, so we put our own desires aside. And this tendency continues for most of us into adulthood.

It's particularly hard for us when the boundaries we want to set go against cultural or familial norms. If you come from a culture or family in which there are few, if any, boundaries, you probably fear that your family will say you're out of line if you try to set one. You might find that other members of your family are appalled that you've broken the "family code" by demanding better behavior from your brother or choosing not to come home for the holidays. I'm not denying it—you are likely to rock a number of boats in the process of becoming a boundary badass. (I certainly have!) But there is no other choice. Putting yourself in a virtual straitjacket and not living the life that was meant for you? That cannot be your fate. You're ready for something different, or you wouldn't be reading this book.

Recently, my client Priya wanted to set a new boundary with her family that she knew wasn't going to be easy. Her family expected her to take a trip with them as she had always done, but she didn't want to join them this time because she knew it would be stressful and full of conflict. When I urged Priya to take a step toward the boundary, she backed away quickly. "I think I'll just do nothing and hope it will be okay," she said.

"How has that worked for you in the past?" I asked her. She had to admit that it hadn't worked out for her at all. Doing nothing is an avoidance tactic; it's the same as saying yes to what we don't want. Ultimately, Priya decided to set the boundary and not take the trip with her family. It was difficult, but she was much happier to do what she wanted with that time.

For those of us who faced substantial conflicts in our childhood homes, however, it can be downright terrifying to feel anger from another human being. So we bend over backward to keep the peace, even if we practically break our own backs doing it.

"When I was about six years old," Renee says, "I witnessed my mother losing her temper with my sister. I remember my mother's face turning red as she picked up a fire poker and ran after my sister. Depending on who is telling the story, my mother either ran into the hallway door or had it slammed in her face. As a result, my mom broke her nose in two places. I cowered in the corner as the scene unfolded. I knew that I never wanted to be on the other end of that fire poker, so from that point on, I was a model child. What I learned from this was it's not okay to go against, push back, or argue with someone, especially someone who could withdraw love from me. If I did, I would get hurt, or someone else would get hurt. I must always comply. This commitment to compliance contributed to my inability to say no to my father when he sexually molested me. I also found it difficult to say no to requests from my children for toys, food, or virtually anything, even if it eventually led to bankruptcy. My mind-set was to avoid conflict at any cost. When someone asked me to jump, I would ask how high—even if my stomach was simultaneously doing somersaults. This continues to affect my decisions. For example, I would like to join a local chorus that has rehearsals the same night as my Toastmasters meetings. I haven't gone to Toastmasters in over a year and have no intention to go back, yet I continue to pay dues because I'm afraid it may upset someone to lose a member."

I recognize that the fear of conflict can be great. It's understandable that Renee's childhood experience was so terrifying to her. But she's an adult now and must learn to stop allowing that childhood terror to rule her life.

When we're afraid to set a boundary, we justify and rationalize the impact that not setting it will have on us. We decide we can "handle it." But many of us have been handling it for years in situations where we should never have been handling it at all! And all along, it takes its toll in the form of buried resentments. But resentment has a way of working itself to the surface, no matter how hard we try to keep it at bay. We might snap at our child or become passive aggressive with our partner or a co-worker, doling out our repressed anger in destructive ways. Over time, we might blow up with rage or, as in my own case, behave in a way that completely demolishes a relationship. As I mentioned earlier, my client Yvonne held on to her anger for so long that she struck her husband and wound up with an assault charge.

When we say yes (or nothing at all) when what we *really* want to say is "No effing way," we end up in a loop where we feel we have to say yes over and over . . . and over. It feels like the easy way out. But trust me—as someone who did that for many years in my marriage—it isn't the easy way out *at all*. It may hold outer conflict at bay for a while, but it amplifies our *inner* conflict tremendously. I want to say that again: we amplify our *inner* conflict when we avoid *outer* conflict with someone else! Since we can't bury our feelings forever, we're just putting off the inevitable. When the truth comes back to haunt us, it comes with claws out. The conflict with the other person is almost always much worse than it would have been had we been honest from the start.

It's funny what lengths we go to on a regular basis to make sure someone else in our life doesn't become angry—only to later become enraged ourselves!

The most natural emotion to feel when our boundary gets crossed is anger. *How dare they do that?* But since anger is seen culturally as unacceptable and dangerous—perhaps especially for women and people of color—we have long been taught to numb it out. We've gotten the message that our anger is dangerous and not to be trusted, so we do everything in our power to avoid expressing it.

But repressing anger is exactly how we set ourselves up to lose control. We can't hold it in anymore, and the next thing we know, we're spewing rage. This is one of the places we have to relearn what we've been taught. Our anger, when expressed mindfully and not dumped on someone else's doorstep, is extremely powerful. The key is to learn to say, "I'm feeling angry"—first to ourselves and later to the people in our lives who need to hear it.

There's a bonus problem that shows up when we keep our anger under lock and key. *Suppressing any feeling requires that we numb ourselves to* all *of our feelings.* There's no way to numb out from anger or sadness without also deleting joy and happiness. The avoidance strategies we use to shut down our negative emotions—drugs, alcohol, food, excessive work, exercise, shopping, mindless Internet surfing (fill in your favorite here)—don't discern the good from the bad.

Our bodies end up holding the bag, keeping track of every feeling we've not allowed ourselves to have. This is why so many of us feel a boundary violation in our body first. Once I started doing the boundary work, I started to notice something unexpected. Whenever I was about to be faced with a choice—whenever I needed to set a boundary—I would feel a strange sensation in the middle of my biceps. It's as if someone had wrapped barbed wire around me from the back to the front, rotating the wire like a twist tie. It comes up when I feel totally restrained; like I have no choice but to violate my own boundary. I now feel the "barbed wire twist tie" whenever I'm out of alignment with what's true for me.

When her sister violated one of her boundaries, my client Candace developed a pinched nerve in her neck. One client feels it in her jaw, while another feels it in his stomach. Elaine feels it as a constriction in her throat, as if her fear is trying to prevent her from saying what she's afraid to say.

Louise Hay used to say if we don't pay attention to our body's whispers, it will eventually let us know how it feels in no uncertain terms. When Renee didn't set boundaries at work, she became increasingly ill, both emotionally and physically. This included depression, anxiety, panic attacks, and suicidal feelings. Physically, she developed adult-onset asthma and Crohn's disease.

We're so accustomed to discounting the warning signs from the body that most humans fail to make the connection between illness and boundaries. We discount our own discomfort, pain, and alarm signals. We stay in a bad situation and continue our overgiving until we can't numb ourselves out anymore. Eventually, our unattended boundaries and the resulting repressed anger can wreak permanent damage on our bodies.

As you contemplate the areas of your life where you aren't setting appropriate limits, you might start to feel down on yourself. You might label yourself as a 100 percent doormat and feel like you're starting from square one. But take heart—all of us know how to set *some* boundaries. Looking at the boundaries we manage to hold easily and effortlessly is the next part of the process.

So before you think about the boundaries you haven't yet been able to set, let's take a quick inventory of the ones you *have*! This exercise will prove to you that boundary setting is not only possible, but is already happening in your life right now.

EXERCISE

Take an Inventory of Boundaries You Easily Hold

In this exercise, you'll write an inventory of boundaries that you easily hold, as well as how you hold each one. You can do this exercise either on paper or on a device of your choice.

1. Think of at least five boundaries you've set in your life, easily and effortlessly, and the ways in which you maintain them. Here are several examples to help you make your own list:

I have a boundary against letting strangers into the house.
How I keep it: I lock the doors and windows.

I have a boundary against being physically harmed.
How I keep it: I wear a seatbelt, avoid riding in a car with an intoxicated driver, and steer clear of people who are violent.

I have a boundary against getting sick.
How I keep it: I refuse to eat foods that cause a negative reaction in my body, I avoid cats since I'm allergic, and I don't take recreational drugs.

I have a boundary against getting my bag stolen.
How I keep it: I keep my bag closed and stay aware of its whereabouts at all times.

I have a boundary against taking part in illegal behavior.
How I keep it: I refuse to participate if someone suggests doing anything illegal.

I have a boundary against my kids staying up late.
How I keep it: I require that they go to bed at a decent hour.

2. This time, take an inventory of the boundaries you've set in each of the following areas of your life:

- Between you and your significant other, if you have one. (For example, you may have a boundary against cheating on each other.)
- Between you and your children, if you have them. (For example, you have probably given your kids a curfew.)
- Between you and your parents, if they're still living.
- Between you and your siblings, if you have any.
- Between you and other family members.
- Between you and your friends.
- Between you and your co-workers.
- Between you and your clients.

Have you discovered that you're a better boundary setter in some areas of your life than you realized? Let this exercise prove to you that you can become better at setting boundaries in the areas that challenge you.

Overdue Boundaries

Now that you know you *do* set at least a few clear boundaries in your life, let's think about the boundaries that you've avoided—the ones that are overdue. These are often a result of trying to avoid conflict at all costs. But avoiding conflict means accepting *long-term discomfort*—sometimes for decades—in order to avoid the *short-term discomfort* of setting a necessary boundary.

Most of us stay unconscious or passive when we allow others to cross our boundaries. We don't take action to prevent the violation. So to set a boundary, we have to make a new, conscious choice to take action. This is especially difficult if we've allowed someone to cross our boundaries for years. To suddenly take a different action than usual is particularly scary because the other person isn't expecting the change—and may not like it.

For example, perhaps you've taken on all of the cleaning responsibilities in your household. You're exhausted and resentful, but you've bitten your tongue for so long that you don't know how else to do it. Maybe you never say no to relatives who just drop by whenever they feel like it, even though it's inconvenient for you. Maybe your boss repeatedly gives you weekend work without extra pay, and you accept it because you fear losing your job.

We choose not to set a needed boundary because we're prioritizing keeping the peace and avoiding the short-term discomfort of potential conflict. While it's easy to think of boundaries as difficult to set, we forget that it's also hard *not* to set a boundary. It takes a lot of energy to endure bad behavior, swallow our resentment, and pretend everything is *fine*. We assume it's better to endure long-term discomfort in silence. But as we've already discussed, there are even more serious consequences when we avoid setting the boundaries we need and want.

Imagine denying your own needs in a relationship because you're afraid the person you love might leave you if you set a boundary. Doing whatever it takes to keep someone from leaving you is a high price to pay for that person's company. Not only are your own needs not getting met, but you're wasting a whole lot of energy walking on eggshells, trying not to upset your partner. You might be able to pretend on the outside that everything is fine, but deep down, you know better.

I know the thought of losing someone you care about can be terrifying—so terrifying that many of us overstay in relationships, hoping a miracle will occur and the other person will see the light. But the hard truth is that if your relationship cannot survive you naming and claiming your needs, what kind of relationship *is* it? If this person won't stay unless you compromise your own needs to such a degree, does the individual truly care about you? I would argue—emphatically—that you are worth more than that. Also, that being alone with your self-respect might be a more satisfying outcome than staying in a relationship in which you feel you have to constantly step on your needs.

If any of this sounds familiar, imagine me putting my hands on your shoulders and looking deeply into your eyes. *You are worthy of someone who wants to be with the real you. It's time to stop abandoning yourself for the sake of another.* If setting a boundary will make or break a relationship, there's a bigger conversation to be had about that relationship.

We're overly "other-referenced," meaning that we concern ourselves with other people's needs far too often, completely negating the negative impact on ourselves. Most of us continue to settle for long-term discomfort until we have a forced life change like in my case or until we pick up a book like this and begin to consciously work on boundaries.

For many of my clients, romantic relationships top the list of areas where boundaries are seriously overdue. That may be you as well. Or your primary issue may lie in work, or with your kids. You may be well aware of the boundaries in this or other areas that are overdue to be set. Or you may be thinking, *I don't even know if I have overdue boundaries.* If the latter feels true, it might be that you're so disconnected from your needs and desires that you aren't aware of where you're allowing your boundaries to be crossed. If that's you, I get it. In my marriage, my husband dictated what I ate, what I wore, and how I exercised. Checking in with my own desires was foreign to me. If someone had asked me what overdue boundaries were on my plate, I would probably have shrugged my shoulders. I quite literally did not see all the pain, anger, and sadness I'd been repressing for years.

One of the ways you can begin to unearth your overdue boundaries is to think of the relationships you fear losing if you take care of your own desires and needs. This will show you how you've been abandoning yourself to buy love or acceptance from others. Similarly, any situation in which you've found yourself complaining or whining (either aloud or silently to yourself) is probably one in which a boundary is overdue.

The exercise that follows will help you sort out these overdue boundaries in your life. Even if you feel you're perfectly aware of the boundaries you need to set, you may discover new ones by going through the steps of this exercise.

EXERCISE

Emotional Inventory and Overdue Boundaries

In this exercise, you'll start by thinking about where in your life you feel negative emotions. Then, you'll look at whether the causes of those emotions are boundaries you've allowed to be crossed. Be sure to write down your answers, whether in a notebook or on a device of your choice.

1. Think about your home and work environment, as well as your interactions with the various people in your life from family to friends to co-workers. Write down the areas and situations that cause you to feel any of the following emotions:

Anger—Do you feel anger in your life? If so, why? If you aren't sure why, ask yourself why someone might feel anger about the circumstances of your life.

- **Fear**—Do you feel fearful in your life? If so, why? If you aren't sure why, ask yourself why someone might feel fearful about the circumstances of your life.

- **Depression**—Do you feel depressed in your life? If so, why? If you aren't sure why, ask yourself why someone might feel depressed about the circumstances of your life.

- **Helplessness**—Do you feel helpless in your life? If so, why? If you aren't sure why, ask yourself why someone might feel helplessness about the circumstances of your life.

- **Hopelessness** and **Apathy**—Do you feel hopeless or apathetic in your life? If so, why? If you aren't sure why, ask yourself why someone might feel hopeless or apathetic about the circumstances of your life.

- **Sadness**—Do you feel sadness in your life? If so, why? If you aren't sure why, ask yourself why someone might feel sadness about the circumstances of your life.

- **Exhaustion**—Do you feel exhausted and drained in your life? If so, why? If you aren't sure why, ask yourself why someone might feel exhausted and drained about the circumstances of your life.

2. Review each circumstance you wrote about in answer to question #1, and write down answers to these questions:

- How might this negative emotion be the result of a crossed boundary?

- How would this situation have to change for me to get what I *really* want?

- What boundary could I set in order to get closer to my desire?

- Have I expressed this boundary clearly to myself and others?

3. Now, review your work and make a list of the boundaries you need but have not set. These are your overdue boundaries.

For example, you might write: "I feel anger toward my sister for putting me down in front of my family. She has been doing this for years. My overdue boundary is to let her know I will leave the next time she puts me down."

Or: "I feel depressed and exhausted because I don't know if my marriage is going to survive. I'm trying so hard to hold my failing marriage together that I never do anything for myself. My overdue boundary is to stop doing everything I can to placate my wife out of the fear of losing her and to make a new commitment to my own joy."

Some of my clients' overdue boundaries include:

- Charging for the work I do, even when my customers expect it for free.

- Requiring my husband treat me with respect.

- No longer giving too much money to my adult children.

- Asking for overtime pay.

- Refusing to disclose private information about my life to my parents and siblings.

This exercise can be a real eye-opener. If you've now discovered that boundaries are causing some of the emotional issues in your life, take heart. As you continue reading, you'll learn strategies for rectifying these ongoing problems.

The Boundary Pyramid

I'm sure you've noticed that not all of your boundaries are created equal, not even your overdue ones. Some hurt you a great deal, and some are just mildly annoying. Others fall somewhere in between.

Here's an example of a mildly annoying boundary: My friend doesn't watch TV. When she's visiting her mother, it drives her bonkers that the television is on all the time, from morning to night. Since it's her mother's home, she doesn't feel right about requesting the TV be turned off entirely, but she did ask for the boundary of turning off the sound during dinner. Her mother would prefer to keep it on (because, *Jeopardy!*), but she agreed. I call this one a "cherry-on-top" boundary. It's one that you'd love to have, but it isn't essential to your well-being.

Then, there are the medium-sized boundaries. These are definitely "good-to-have" limits that would make your life easier and more pleasant. For example, your dear friend sends you several texts during the day and expects you to answer quickly. You simply don't have time to interrupt your work so often to respond to her texts, and you'd like to ask her to not send them during the workday unless they're urgent. This isn't dire, but it's causing you to feel some resentment toward your friend. Another possibility is a situation at work in which people gather around the watercooler right outside your office and talk so loudly that even with your door closed, it's hard to concentrate on your important phone conversations. In this situation, you want to ask the group of co-workers to keep their voices down when outside your office.

Finally, there are your bottom-line boundaries—the ones you're most afraid to set but which are way past due. These are the behaviors you will no longer tolerate. If they persist, you will take action to protect yourself in some way, even if it means removing yourself from the situation. For example, maybe your husband insists on getting into political arguments with your father whenever they're together, and this causes you a great deal of stress. Once you tell him how you feel when this happens, you will let him know that you'll leave the room or the house if he does it again.

One of my bottom-line boundaries is that I absolutely need and want to meditate immediately after I wake up. So I set a boundary with my partner that I won't communicate with him until after I finish my meditation. Other bottom-line boundaries for me include not smoking in my house and not accepting mean-spirited criticism. My friend Anna has the bottom-line boundary that she won't remain in the room when her brother-in-law goes into one of his classic fits of rage, while my client Alex's bottom-line boundary involves refusing to answer his sister's nosy questions about his personal life.

Don't worry—I'm not asking you to set any of these boundaries *yet*. This step is just to make an inventory. It's your chance to evaluate where you are with boundaries before you venture into setting them. Remember: You do *not* have to set any boundary that doesn't feel comfortable for you; everyone has their own timeline and their own process. But it's important to write down the boundaries that you *would* set if you felt like you could. This is a critical moment in the process, so don't shortchange yourself. Be brave; write down every unset boundary you can think of.

On the other hand, you may be champing at the bit to set that one big bottom-line boundary now that you're starting to feel permission to do so. My recommendation is to take a pause and wait until we get to Steps 7 to 9 before starting to set any as-yet unspoken limits. It's especially important not to jump right to one of your bottom-line boundaries until you read further. The chapters that follow will not only help you develop the courage to set your boundaries, but they'll set you up for a greater chance of success.

EXERCISE

Your Boundary Pyramid

For this exercise, go back to your list of overdue boundaries, and let's divide them up into their appropriate categories.

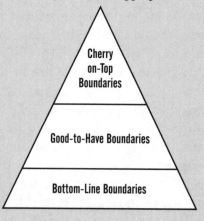

1. Which would you consider cherry-on-top boundaries? Add them to the top of your pyramid. These boundaries aren't difficult to set, but they feel like a bit of a reach. They are the "I couldn't

really have it *that* good, could I?" boundaries. For example, this kind of boundary might be altering the thermostat in your bedroom for your comfort at night or having quiet time from 6 to 7 P.M. when your kids get home from school.

2. Which would you consider good-to-have boundaries—the ones that would make your life significantly better? Add them to the middle of your pyramid. For example, this kind of boundary might be no longer taking calls from your brother after 8 P.M. or asking your neighbors to keep their garbage cans off your property.

3. Which are your bottom-line boundaries? These are the ones that cause you the most long-term discomfort—the ones you would set today if you weren't afraid to do so. For example, these might include no longer doing all the cleaning in the house or walking away when your mother starts to tell you what she believes you've been doing wrong in your life.

Hold on to your Boundary Pyramid, as you'll refer back to it several times during the course of reading the book.

Now that you have your Boundary Pyramid, you have a good sense of the limits you need to set in your life. You'll discover more as you keep reading, but first we need to move on to Step 3. This is where we'll begin to tackle some of the emotional obstacles we face when trying to set boundaries.

REMEMBER

You may experience some consequences as a result of setting boundaries, but there are also consequences from *not* setting boundaries.

CONQUER CODEPENDENCE

"As a little kid, I walked on eggshells and took the temperature of the room before deciding how to feel or act," Jessica says. "This is still true with my dad. Even on the phone, I can tell before he says hello how it's going to go. Is this 'Good Mood Don' or 'Cranky Don' or someone else entirely? It has been so toxic that I literally got the shingles once when I decided to confront him. I'd love to say I'm over it and not triggered by him, but it isn't true. Just thinking of planning a trip to see him involves strategizing, and my sister and I still play this codependent game of 'Did you tell Dad?' We keep information from him out of fear of how he'll react or simply because we don't want to 'deal' with him."

Tina says she squashed her own needs if her husband felt uncomfortable doing something she wanted to do. Then, she simply stopped asking for what she wanted. "I stopped doing things I loved because he didn't want to do them," she says. "My husband doesn't like bars. When I met him, all my friends were in bands, and even though

I didn't drink, I was in bars all the time to sing or watch my friends perform. Eventually, I disconnected from my friends because it wasn't what my husband wanted to do. I see the pattern of how I continually gave up parts of me and became resentful. While I can take ownership that I chose those things, it's a hard reality to face."

Valerie's childhood set her up for her own needs to be negated, and it has continued into her adulthood until now, when she's learning how to take her own desires into account and set much-needed boundaries in her life.

These are examples of codependency—behavior in which we habitually put the needs of others ahead of our own. I define *codependency* as looking for someone outside of us to emotionally regulate us. In other words, we don't know our own mood until we find out the mood of others around us.

We often think a codependent person is someone who enables an addict of some kind, but that isn't necessarily the case. Many of us are codependent, even though we have no addictive people in our lives. Like Jessica, we check the emotional temperature of others around us before we check our own emotions. But that's backward! We need to learn to check in with our *own* emotions and desires *before* we check everyone else's.

Why are we codependent? It helps us feel safe. We think, *I'll check in with their opinion first, and then I'll have a sense of my own opinion.* The idea is that if we know what opinions are acceptable to others, we won't run the risk of being ridiculed or abandoned for our own opinion. I did this for years, not just in my marriage but in every relationship in my life.

Codependent behavior is one of the main reasons many of us fail to set boundaries in our lives. That's why Step 3 in this process requires us to *Conquer Codependence.*

Codependence and Boundaries

Having a desire separate from others can feel foreign to those of us who are extreme codependents. Often, when asked what we want, we automatically flash to what *others* want. Our desire becomes less about our own well-being than about whatever it takes to stay safe in relation to other people.

As codependent people, we're empathic. We "take on" the energy of others, so boundaries can be particularly shaky for us. We struggle to tell where our feelings end and others' begin. When something happens to someone we love, it feels like it's happening to *us.* We work hard to make sure everyone around us is okay, while paying little attention to whether or not *we're* okay. We tell ourselves we're protecting other people from negative emotions or consequences, but we end up swallowing the poison ourselves.

The result? We overstep our own boundaries to take care of the other person, keep the peace, and maintain connection. We say yes when we don't really agree, and if someone asks us what we truly want, we aren't even sure. For many of us, this even means tolerating abusive behavior.

This shows up in large and small ways. For example, a friend of mine often accepts less than satisfying massages because she can't bear to make a request for something different. She's too worried the massage therapist will feel criticized, and she can't bring herself to cause someone else even this minor amount of discomfort. Meanwhile, it probably wouldn't affect the therapist at all if she simply asked for an adjustment in the pressure. Even if the comment *did* activate some insecurity on the part of the massage therapist, as an adult, it's that person's responsibility to deal with those feelings.

Most of us become codependent in childhood. We felt we had to walk on eggshells, as Jessica said, checking in with the feelings of others and acting accordingly for self-preservation. This set us up to be hypersensitive to the moods of others, and we've become very talented at molding ourselves into whatever others have needed us to be.

Codependent behavior is actually a strong compulsion to control situations for safety's sake. My friend Marcia's mother, for example, did all of Marcia's brother's homework for him because she was so afraid he might fail. As a result, he grew up without confidence in his own abilities. To their mother, however, it was an effort to control a situation that frightened her. Of course, when we behave codependently, we're trying to control something that's actually *outside* of our control: someone else's experience.

Not to mention that codependency isn't sustainable. It's based solely on fear of the opinions of others—which is no way to live. Plus, it's dishonest and inauthentic. We can only put ourselves on the back burner for so long— eating the scraps and crumbs while handing off the juicy meal to others. Eventually, the overgiving catches up to us. Our true self wants its fair share. It wants to break out so that we can be who we really are and reach our potential in life. No matter how hard we may try to deny it, we all have a compulsion to be authentic and to balance how much we give to others with how much we give to ourselves. It's one of the lessons we're here to learn.

Changing our codependent tendencies requires that we become aware of our own desires and needs. Then, we have to learn how to stay with those desires and needs rather than allow them to be altered by anyone else's feelings or wants. It took me a long time to get to a point where I could maintain my own good mood around others regardless of what they were feeling. Now, I can stay anchored in how I feel even when someone else is feeling down or angry.

To start becoming aware of our codependent behavior, we must learn to catch ourselves if we get caught up in someone else's drama or make someone else's desires more important than our own. It takes vigilance and awareness. We have to pay attention to our behaviors in order to notice when we put others first without considering our own needs. Awareness is the first step toward giving ourselves the nurturing we need before focusing on the nurturing of others.

Jessica is beginning to alter her codependent behavior. Her sister texted her one day upset about an attorney bill she owed that she could not pay. "The old me would have immediately offered to put the amount on my credit card with the hope that my sister would pay me in installments," she says. "Instead, I wrote her back saying I was sorry to hear that and asked if she'd requested installment payments. She responded that she was sure everything would work out 'somehow.' Part of me still feels bad, but I haven't backtracked. The benefit has been a feeling of self-respect and not having a debt of thousands of dollars on my credit card!"

It may sound like a lot of work to alter these habitual behaviors in which you put others ahead of yourself, but the difference in your life will be enormous. Everyone I know who has grown up codependent and later embarked on the journey of healing has improved the quality of their lives to an incalculable degree.

The following is just one way in which my client Paula's life improved when she conquered her codependent patterns. "When my son Paul was in elementary school, he saw his dad Robert every other weekend," she says. "That amount of time was not enough for Paul. He missed his dad between visits, and sometimes his hurt feelings/ missing his dad would come out sideways as misbehavior. I used to call Robert and remind him to call Paul. Then, his dad would call, Paul would be happy, and so would I. After working on my codependent tendencies, I realized I was trying to control what kind of parent Robert was by telling him when to contact Paul and what method to use. I had expectations for Robert to be more involved in Paul's life and was trying to make him behave as I expected he should. I realized that no matter how much I tried to control the situation, Paul would have to deal with his hurt feelings at some point. So I stopped asking Robert to call his son. I knew initially it would be challenging for Paul, but in the long run, it would be better for all involved. Eventually, as Paul got older, he and his dad figured out their own communication schedule and method. The impact for me personally was *less* stress!"

In my book *Permission to Put Yourself First,* I introduced this radical thought: *We can still care about another person without "taking on" their emotions or problems.* This is hard for codependents to fathom, but it's true. As Paula discovered, we can even do this in relation to our children. Now, that's really a radical thought! While we are indeed responsible for the well-being of our kids, it is not our responsibility to shield them from life. And life, as it turns out, includes lots of feelings and experiences, both positive and negative.

Detaching from the needs of others does not mean detaching from our love for them, however. When we behave as if our loved ones are incapable of taking care of themselves without our intervention, we are infantilizing them. This is not good for anyone! Instead, we can become aware of where we're overdoing, overgiving, and relieving others of their own responsibilities. Then, we can set necessary boundaries to take care of *ourselves*—and let others take responsibility for their own well-being.

Self-Denial and Guilt

Wondering if you might have the codependence disease? Look for one of its most common symptoms: guilt. When we believe it's our duty to keep everyone else happy, we tend to feel guilty that we even *have* our own needs and desires.

Valerie was taught this in the extreme. "When I'm choosing me and doing what I want, I feel guilt and shame," she says. "I've had to lie about or hide the things that are really important to me in life." Her parents split up when she was a child, and her mother disapproved of Valerie's love for her father. So painful as it was, in order to feel accepted by her mother, Valerie cut her father out of her life and tried to disconnect from her love for him. Since that incident happened at such a young, impressionable age, she has grown up believing that honoring her own feelings is wrong. "When I've mustered up the courage to make a choice for me, I have felt like I was a terrible person, hurting others in the process." Most of the time, of course, no one else has even been affected by her choices, let alone hurt. For example, Valerie has felt wrong for turning down gatherings with friends, but no one has thought anything of her deciding not to join them. When we develop beliefs like these at such a young age, they remain powerful forces in our lives until we become aware of them and question them consciously.

As my client Mary was doing the boundary work, she battled lots of guilt. Specifically, she needed to set some boundaries with her parents, who expected her to listen to their problems several times a week. The negativity was having a substantial impact on her health, but telling them she would no longer be available for those conversations made her feel terrible. Nevertheless, the guilt she felt was just a reminder of how she had overstepped her own boundaries her whole life. As Mary becomes more comfortable taking care of herself—and allowing others to take responsibility for themselves—the guilt will subside.

Guilt is natural, and it also isn't the end of the world. We can feel guilty and still hold the boundaries that are right for us. Feeling guilty has become a habit—a safety mechanism keeping us stuck with the status quo. It isn't an indicator that we're doing anything wrong. In fact, it's a sign that we're doing something right! How's this for another radical thought:

> *If you feel guilty while setting*
> *a boundary, it's good news!*
> *It means you're finally breaking old*
> *patterns and honoring yourself.*

Guilt is the normal experience of changing the rules with the people we love. But it's tolerable and survivable.

Many years ago, before I learned this important truth, I was with Louise Hay in London during a Hay House event. Louise wanted me to visit some gardens with her, but I was exhausted. I mustered up my courage to take care of myself first, and I actually said no to Louise. *I said no to Louise Hay!* This wasn't at all a big deal to her, but it was a *huge* deal to me at the time. I felt so guilty. But what I know now is that the guilt was good news because this was a big turning point for me. By taking care of myself rather than automatically saying yes to someone who meant so much to me, I was learning how to nurture myself. And I was learning that just because I felt guilty, it wasn't my responsibility to fix someone else's disappointment.

Something I always find funny is that we codependent types demand self-sacrifice from ourselves, but rarely ask it of others! If we did, the give-to-receive ratio in our relationships would be in balance; we would not have room to always be overgiving but would instead be open to receiving. It's kind of self-important, the way we insist to the universe that the responsibility to care for others is solely on our own shoulders. Why do we think *we're* so very special?

As I've said many times, when we deny our own needs long enough, they come out sideways. By *sideways*, I mean that our needs express themselves either through unconscious behaviors or via illness (whether mental or physical). In some cases, life forces us to make a change unexpectedly—our partner asks for a divorce, we get fired from our job, our house burns down, or we total our car. As seemingly random as these events may be, they can act as useful wake-up calls toward deeper reflection about how we're choosing to live our lives. Are we taking good enough care of ourselves? Are we heeding the warnings our bodies and hearts are sending us? And are we making our own happiness and fulfillment our first priority? If not, something needs to change.

To do that, however, we need to step into a greater sense of our own worth. As our sense of worthiness increases, we grow less and less comfortable with taking the crumbs and not getting the whole meal. In this way, self-worth, codependency, and boundaries are strongly related to each other. When we feel worthy, we *know* we deserve as much as everyone else, and we want to see to it that we receive it. As research professor and best-selling author Brené Brown put it: "Only when we believe, deep down, that we *are* enough can we say 'Enough!'"

When I first started to work on my self-worth and boundary setting, my then therapist gave me a rope and had me sit on the floor. She asked me to place the rope around me to denote what I perceived to be my personal space. I placed the rope as close to my body as I could and hugged my knees tightly to my chest, making myself as small as possible. In other words, I had almost no personal space in which to move, breathe, and feel safe. All of my personal space had been relinquished to others. That rope on the floor was a moment for me, let me tell you. I saw in a visible way how much I was sacrificing to live as a people pleaser.

In the book *Codependent No More,* author Melody Beattie writes: "I used to spend so much time reacting and respond-ing to everyone else that my life had no direction. Other people's lives, problems, and wants set the course for my life. Once I realized it was okay for me to think about and identify what I wanted, remarkable things began to take place in my life."

I so relate to that. I can't even begin to quantify or describe how much more I enjoy my life now than in the past. Today, my life is of my own design, and it's on my own terms. I don't say yes to anyone until I know what I want, and I make my desires my first priority. On a daily basis, I make decisions based on what I want and need, and I trust that the other people in my life will take care of what they want and need. I don't give in, acquiesce, or accommodate. If what I want means I have to say no, then I say no. I fully understand now that someone else's reaction to my truth is not my responsibility to manage. When I'm generous, it's because I feel a genuine desire to give. It isn't about trying to stay out of trouble or get someone to like me. This is a portrait of what healing codependence and learning how to set boundaries can be like for you.

EXERCISE

Where Is Codependency Getting in the Way of Your Boundaries?

This exercise consists of two parts. First, you'll assess if you're codependent. Then, you'll explore how your codependency is affecting your ability to set boundaries. Write down your answers to all of the questions, either in a journal or on a device.

Part 1: Are You Codependent in Relationships?

1. Answer these questions about your tendencies in relationships:

- Have you often felt you were the only one making an effort in your relationships?

- Do you feel you don't have enough time for yourself?

- Do you frequently feel that your partners and others in your life don't know how to accomplish tasks correctly or satisfactorily?

- Do people in your life tend to rely on you to make plans and take care of details?

- Have you ever found yourself stuck in a relationship, unable to break away emotionally?

- Do you frequently hold back your feelings because you're afraid of hurting someone else or making the person angry?

- Do you struggle to let others know when they've hurt your feelings or done something insensitive?

- Do you find it difficult to say no when someone asks you for help?

- Do you often feel overwhelmed with all you've promised to do for others?

- Do you believe it's courteous to let others make decisions, even when the decisions will affect you?

If you answered *yes* to any of these questions, you probably struggle with codependency to at least some degree. For any yes answers, make a list of the different ways you may have crossed your own boundaries in relation to that question. For example, if you said yes to "feeling overwhelmed with all you've promised to do for others," you might write down something like this: "I crossed my boundary when I accepted the PTA president role even though I didn't really have time."

Part 2: How Your Codependency Affects Your Boundaries

1. Make a list of the people you tend to care for the most in your life. They are probably family members or close friends.

2. Next to each person's name, write down anything you regularly do for them that, if you're honest, they could probably do themselves.

3. By taking on these responsibilities, what boundaries are you allowing to be crossed in each of these relationships? Take notes for each person on your list.

4. If you have discovered new overdue boundaries through this exercise, add them to their proper places on your Boundary Pyramid from the last chapter (Step 2).

When *You're* on the Other Side
of Someone's Boundary

In this book, we're focusing on the boundaries that we need to set with others, but we have all inevitably crossed others' boundaries as well. Can you remember a time when someone set a strong boundary with you? How did it feel? If it felt uncomfortable, it may have reinforced your belief that setting boundaries with others is not okay. Can you reframe that experience in your mind, now that you understand more about the importance of boundary setting?

Ironically, our overgiving tendencies can sometimes cause us to cross boundaries we don't even know are there. My client Paula recalls a time when she accompanied a friend who was buying a couch at a furniture store: "She financed it, and I asked some specific questions about the terms of the contract. My friend looked at me and said, 'That's none of your business.' She was absolutely right. I apologized and stopped asking questions. I remember this scenario when I feel tempted to meddle in a codependent way, and it reminds me to check myself to make sure I'm staying in my own lane."

Paula was trying to help by asking the right questions, but in the process, she unintentionally infantilized her friend, as if this grown woman wasn't capable of handling her own couch purchase. This is one of the classic ways that codependent types inadvertently step on the boundaries of others.

Let's Redefine Selfishness and Self-Respect

Selfishness has a bad rep that it simply doesn't deserve. I'm not talking about the kind of selfishness that means you step on everyone *else's* boundaries and don't care if you hurt others. I'm not talking about an excuse to treat others poorly. But I do think our society thinks of selfishness as uniformly "bad," leading many of us to deny ourselves the self-love and self-respect we deserve.

It has been a long time coming for me, but I now assume that what's best for me is what's best for any relationship I'm in—whether it's with my significant other, a family member, a friend, or someone I encounter in business. If I step on my own boundaries for the sake of someone else, I know I will feel resentful. And I know that resentment would be more damaging to the relationship than avoiding whatever short-term conflict the boundary might create.

Believe me, I have tested this out over the past few years. What I've discovered is that, when we're all aligned with our own best interests, we all get more of what we want. I'm talking about reasonable interests, of course, which would never include doing harm to others. Harmful behaviors would never be in my best interest or anyone else's.

I'm also not suggesting that I never extend myself outside of my comfort zone in order to help someone else. As I mentioned earlier, I find that the less I feel *obligated* to take care of others, the more I *want* to help them and love them. But I no longer give out of a sense of responsibility for someone else or the need to prove anything. When I give, I do so from a genuine desire. My gift is no longer tainted with resentment or need.

It's clean—without the requirement of getting anything in return. And it replenishes me; it doesn't drain me.

I think of selfishness, self-care, and self-love as three sisters, whose job it is to support us in honoring ourselves. If you take care of your own needs and set a boundary, pleasing yourself first, you might end up disappointing someone. *But there's nothing wrong with that.* Connection is more important than consensus. Most of us believe that we must agree in order to stay connected, to stay in relationship. But this is simply not the case. Disagreement and difference is a part of every relationship, and disagreement doesn't mean disconnection.

Each person has the responsibility to take care of one's own needs. Heck, when your partner, sibling, or co-worker sets a boundary, it may be *you* who's disappointed in the process! But that's okay too. Most relationships can survive disappointment. What our relationships cannot survive is long-term overgiving and the resentment that results from it.

We must simply cultivate the skill of disagreeing without making the other person wrong. This allows us to have our boundaries and stay connected—even when one or both of us ends up feeling disappointed.

Taking care of ourselves and setting the boundaries we need to care for ourselves doesn't have to mean we hurt or deny someone else. It doesn't have to be *either/or.* It can be *both/and.* Often, we can take care of ourselves, and others can also get what they want. Not always, of course, but it can happen more often than we think it can.

The place my clients struggle most with naming and acknowledging difference and disappointment is with their romantic partners. For some reason (cough—fairy tales and rom-coms—cough), we think that a harmonious relationship requires us to agree on everything. When we have a difference around a topic we deem important, we leap to the conclusion that we were never meant to be together. Let me burst the romantic bubble: people disagree. That includes you and your partner.

For a relationship to survive, it needs to have a strong enough foundation to hold the truth of who each person is—even (and especially) when there are differences. It isn't possible for a relationship to be harmonious all the time unless one partner or the other denies the truth of who they are.

So what does a self-responsible, honest relationship look like? Here's one example: In my relationship with Aaron, I craved more alone time, while Aaron simultaneously craved more time together. First, I tuned in to myself and recognized my desire for the alone time. Then, I had to set my boundary with Aaron, letting him know that I would go to my office and close the door three mornings a week rather than have coffee with him, even though I knew he cherished that time with me.

It wasn't easy for me to set that boundary, and Aaron was disappointed. But I put my own needs before his comfort. I made myself a priority. I was sad that he was disappointed, but I knew it wasn't healthy for me to abandon my needs simply to avoid his discomfort and disappointment. He's an adult who can handle those feelings.

In the long run, Aaron came to enjoy the time he had to himself those three mornings a week, so it worked out best for both of us. It was a both/and situation, not an either/or.

There are ways that you can both get your needs met, and I contend that the best way is for you to make yourself a priority, taking responsibility for your own needs, while the other person takes responsibility for theirs. Then, you can just take pleasure in spending time together without the expectations that so often lead to conflict—the very conflict that we're trying desperately, as codependent people, to avoid. We'd have much more success avoiding that conflict if we took responsibility for ourselves and put ourselves in the number-one priority position. We would automatically set healthy boundaries on a regular basis, and everyone would be happier and healthier for it.

The most important thing I can say to you, particularly if you lean toward codependency, is to learn to stay true to yourself. Discover who you are, what you want, and how you want your life to look. Then, you can make choices and set boundaries based on those desires rather than on the desires of others.

"In the past, my decisions were based on pleasing the other person or people," my client Bob says. He has mistakenly believed that being a gentleman means making sure others get what they want, while sacrificing what he wants. For example, he might relinquish his own desires when planning evenings out, family vacations, or joint purchases with his wife. Now, he says he's focusing on how *he* will or will not benefit—how the decision will impact *him*, not how he can satisfy the other person. If he doesn't want to go antiquing with his wife on the weekend, he will say so rather than just go along and secretly resent it.

Making yourself a priority is a revolutionary thought for those of us who are codependent. So I have a challenge for you: What if you made your own joy a priority for just one day? If that's too difficult, try it for one hour and extend it until you become more accustomed to checking in with your own desires and making them—at the very least—as important as the desires of others around you (even your children).

What would it look like to prioritize your own needs and your own joy on a regular basis? Here's a snapshot of a day in the life of a non-codependent person:

You wake up in the morning and leave your phone on airplane mode. The first hour of your day is all about you connecting with yourself. You meditate, write in your journal, take a long, hot shower, and eat a healthy breakfast. Instead of rushing to answer e-mails, you feel happy and centered as you begin your day.

When you turn on your phone, you discover that your brother has sent you a text message, telling you he's panicked about being able to make his bills this month. In the past, you would have responded immediately and offered to give him a loan. But you've learned that he overspends, repeatedly creating these financial crises. So you decide you'll answer later when you know exactly what you want to say, but whatever you say, it won't involve offering to help him out of the situation.

But no longer. Today, you speak your truth and hold your boundaries without anger or guilt.

You feel slightly nervous that the individual will be disappointed or upset, but you also feel strong.

As a result, you have an honest dialogue and come to an agreement that feels like a win-win for everyone. (Who knew this was even possible?)

You have an important meeting later in the day (an interview, conversation with a potential client, or a date)—the kind of thing that used to make you try and show up as the "best" version of yourself, putting on a smile in order to be liked. Now, you see this pattern clearly and make a different choice.

You show up as your authentic self, quirks and all. And they *love* it. You even discover that the qualities you felt most insecure about are the ones they like most about you.

If you could go back in time, you'd tell your past self that it can be this way. It's okay to shine, speak up, and be true to yourself. You really can have the life you deserve. But the important thing is that you know it now, and it just keeps getting better.

Does this sound like a fantasy? I promise you it isn't! And it starts with letting go of codependent habits and learning to set healthy boundaries.

EXERCISE
Meditation to Transform Guilt

The next time you feel guilt pulling you back into the whirl-pool of codependence, try this meditation. It will help you sep-arate yourself from others and give them back responsibility for their own well-being.

In preparation, be sure to turn off all phones so that you can surrender to the process. Wear unrestricting clothes, and sit in a comfortable chair or couch. Feel free to play soft music or light candles, if you like. It helps to record your own voice read-ing the steps so that you don't have to open your eyes, which will disrupt your meditative state. If so, you may wish to skip over the italicized portions of the meditation when you record.

Note that the opening part of the meditation will be the same for all meditations to come throughout the book. This is so you can become accustomed to the relaxation portion and make moving into a meditative state second nature.

1. Close your eyes, and take several deep breaths. Relax each part of your body, starting with your feet. Then gradually move up your legs, hips, belly, chest, back, arms, neck, and head until you feel fully relaxed. *Don't work too hard at this. Just ask your body to relax. As you continue, it will relax more and more.*

2. Imagine that you have a cord connecting your solar plexus—the flat area in the center of your torso between your bottom ribs—with the solar plexus of the person whose feelings you feel responsible for. This area is where your emotional chakra is located.

3. Visualize yourself cutting the cord with an imaginary pair of scissors, and as you do, place this other person in the hands of their higher self—the wisest part of them, which is connected to universal wisdom.

4. When you do this, do you feel like you're abandoning this person? Does guilt come up for you? If so, take deep breaths and remind yourself that this individual is capable of self-care and self-responsibility.

5. Imagine that this person's higher self is waving to you and endorsing your desire to set your boundary and no longer take responsibility for anyone else.

6. To reinforce your separation from this person and your acceptance that they can take care of themselves, imagine a cocoon of protective white light circling your body in a spiral from head to toe. This cocoon will keep you as a separate entity from others so that you don't become so enmeshed in their emotions and needs.

7. Also, imagine a cocoon of protective white light circling the body of the other person in a spiral from head to toe. This cocoon will keep them separate from you with their own emotions and needs as their responsibility.

8. When you're ready, wiggle your toes and fingers, and roll your neck to bring yourself back to waking consciousness. Open your eyes, and know

that you have relinquished responsibility for this other person.

9. If the guilt continues, remember that it's a positive indication of the changes you're making. Each time the guilt threatens to prevent you from setting a boundary, close your eyes and cut the cord again, as you also visualize your individual cocoons of light.

Healing codependency is a vital part of learning to set boundaries, which leads you to dig even deeper to discover more emotional obstacles that might stand in your way. With that, you're ready to move on to Step 4 and begin to excavate your unconscious mind.

REMEMBER

If you feel guilty while setting a boundary, it's good news! It means you're finally breaking old patterns and honoring yourself.

EXCAVATE YOUR UNCONSCIOUS MIND

Scientists estimate that 95 percent of the mind's activity is unconscious. This means that the majority of our emotions and behaviors are driven by the unconscious, rather than consciously aware, part of our mind. Is it any surprise, then, that we often don't know why we feel or behave as we do? Why we so frequently eschew choices we *know* would benefit us, favoring those that cause us trouble? No wonder we frequently struggle and feel out of control in our relationships.

The more we're able to bring the unconscious mind's material into conscious awareness, the healthier we become. The more we see, the less likely we are to operate from the hidden fears and issues that prevent us from setting boundaries. Instead, we can take conscious control of asserting what we want and need.

I have already mentioned limiting beliefs, which we sometimes call "shadow beliefs." These beliefs, formed when we were very young, often remain unconscious until we make an effort to bring them to our conscious awareness. Even though beliefs are malleable and revisable, we operate in our adult lives as if our beliefs are just the facts of life.

Over years of doing my own shadow work, I discovered that when I was just two years old, I developed the belief that I have to be perfect in order to be safe. Perfection in my mind meant people-pleasing, which made it nearly impossible for me to set boundaries. As illogical as my belief may have been—and as young as I was when it took up residence in my psyche—it successfully ran the show until just a few years ago!

A friend of mine was reprimanded as a child for expressing anger. As a result, she grew up with the belief that it was wrong to become angry. This has kept her from expressing displeasure about anything, which in turn, has prevented her from setting boundaries.

Neither of these beliefs are facts: anger isn't wrong, and we don't have to be perfect to be safe. But my friend and I both operated in our lives as if these ideas were facts—and they caused us to behave in opposition to what we wanted and needed. Through becoming aware of these shadow beliefs, we were able to install new, healthier beliefs in our psyche's "operating system" so that we could set boundaries and get our needs met.

Besides limiting beliefs, there are other obstacles in the unconscious mind that we need to explore and excavate in order to get past our aversion to setting boundaries. In this step, you'll do just that—dig deep and discover what hidden lines of "code" are standing in the way of setting the boundaries on your pyramid.

Underlying Commitments

One of the most powerful concepts that I learned from my late mentor Debbie Ford, best-selling author and personal transformation teacher, is that we all have "underlying commitments" (sometimes called "unconscious commitments" or "hidden commitments"). According to Debbie, what we *think* or *say* we're committed to is often at odds with a deeper commitment held in our unconscious. So we believe we want one thing, but we're secretly committed to its opposite.

Underlying commitments originated as promises we made to ourselves in childhood, usually as a result of a limiting belief. For example, if you believe, as I did, that you have to be perfect in order to be safe, you might make an unconscious, underlying commitment to do everything possible to be perfect. When, as an adult, you want to set a boundary with someone that goes against your definition of perfect behavior, you will struggle. These commitments explain the disconnect between what we say we *want* to do and what we *actually* do.

One of my other underlying commitments was to make sure I was loved through "earning" my worth. This was based on my belief that I wasn't worthy if I didn't take care of everyone else's needs. So even though I *said* I wanted a relationship with a powerful, self-sufficient man with a steady income, I ended up marrying someone who was dependent on me financially. By taking care of him economically, a part of me believed I was earning my worth as a human being. This underlying commitment became an excuse to stay in my marriage, even though I had to cross my own boundaries repeatedly to do it.

Tina decided it was finally time to separate from her husband. Since they were still living in the same house, she set a boundary with him that they would have no physical contact. "After many months, I crossed my own boundary by sleeping with him because of my need for sex and physical connection," she says. "It's clear to me that I had an underlying commitment to take what I could get, where I could get it. This prevented me from putting myself out there with someone new for fear of rejection, which looped back to the belief that I'm not worthy of my needs being met in a healthy way. So I have just done what's familiar and safe, even though it's not fulfilling."

When Anna was a child, she believed she wouldn't be loved unless she stayed quiet and submissive. Unbeknownst to her, she made an underlying commitment to stay quiet in order to fit in. "The irony is that I never felt like I fit in, because I couldn't express myself," she says. Of course, staying quiet and submissive meant never setting boundaries.

"I won't rock the boat" is another common underlying commitment of those of us who struggle to set boundaries. This may have originated with frightening conflicts in our childhood home or a severe punishment for losing our temper.

Here's another example: Let's say you hate your job and want to set a boundary with your boss to no longer work overtime without pay—yet you just can't seem to make the request. Your unconscious commitment to avoid risk is outweighing your conscious desire to be compensated fairly.

Perhaps you have a belief that you aren't safe when someone is mad at you. As a result, you have an underlying commitment to never make anyone else angry. In order to keep this commitment, you will go out of your way to agree with others and acquiesce to their wishes—keeping totally silent about what *you* want.

In this way, we become so accustomed to "taking the hit" in order to take care of everyone else that we fail to realize how much we're betraying ourselves in the process. Many of us even pride ourselves on our ability to endure these "hits." (I'm talking to you, codependent martyrs of the world!)

If you've been putting off setting a boundary, chances are an underlying commitment is standing in the way. To the children we were, these commitments felt like our best defense against getting hurt. As adults, however, the commitments themselves end up hurting us.

Unfortunately, underlying commitments aren't always easy to puzzle out. Sometimes, what you think you're committed to isn't directly related to your underlying commitment. Here are three examples:

"I *think* I'm committed to making more money and working fewer hours."

Underlying commitment: "I'm actually committed to never rocking the boat, so I stay in my current job even though I'm miserable." (Note that this underlying commitment has nothing to do with making money.)

"I *think* I'm committed to speaking up for myself about what I want."

Underlying commitment: "I'm actually committed to making sure everyone else is always happy." (Note that this underlying commitment has nothing to do with speaking up.)

"I *think* I'm committed to taking good care of myself."

Underlying commitment: "I'm actually committed to fitting in with a daring and unconventional crowd, so I join my friends in their risky behavior."

Some of our underlying commitments are so illogical that they're hard to believe. My client Noele came to realize that she had an underlying commitment to stay miserable. Why would anyone have a commitment to such a thing? While Noele isn't sure, we can speculate that she was surrounded by unhappy adults as a child. We learn what we see, so now feeling miserable is a way to fit in with her family of origin. Perhaps when she was happy, the people around her didn't respond well. Regardless where it came from, the fact is that until recently, Noele has been committed to being miserable like everyone else in her family. Playing the role of the unhappy victim has its benefits. It allows us to avoid taking responsibility for what happens to us, always blaming others for the boundaries we don't set. (It also gives us a very compelling victim story to tell at dinner parties.)

Some underlying commitments can be disengaged quickly, while others are more tenacious. It might be helpful to work with a therapist or coach who is familiar with this concept to both help you figure out your commitments and then overcome them. Just be patient with yourself! Exploring the unconscious mind is lifelong work, but it's also fascinating and exciting, as it allows you to improve the quality of your life more and more with every new discovery.

EXERCISE

Excavate Your Limiting Beliefs and Underlying Commitments

This exercise will help you begin to excavate your underlying commitments. It might take time to figure out these commitments, so be patient. Write down your answers in a journal or on a device of your choice. You might be surprised by some of your answers!

Part 1: Possible Underlying Commitments

1. Review your Boundary Pyramid, and choose the most pressing and difficult boundary you want to set. Then, write the conscious reason you haven't set this boundary, followed by the possible limiting belief(s) and underlying commitment(s) that might be in your way.

Here are some examples:

- **Example #1:**

Boundary I want to set: Telling my brother I will no longer accept him telling me what to do with my life.

Why I don't set this boundary/the belief that holds me back: I believe setting the boundary will cause me to lose my brother.

Possible underlying commitments: I'm committed to making sure I'm not abandoned and alone. I'm committed to avoiding conflict at all costs.

- **Example #2:**

Boundary I want to set: I want to stop taking responsibility for all of my best friend's problems.

Why I don't set a boundary/the belief that holds me back: I believe it's cruel when I say no to my friend's requests, and if I'm cruel, I'm a bad person.

Possible underlying commitment: I'm committed to living up to my definition of a "good person" because if I don't, I'll feel unworthy.

2. Reread your answers. Does the underlying commitment you wrote down ring true for you? If you wrote more than one, which one feels truest for you? Usually, the one that feels right causes us to feel emotional or have an aha moment. If you don't feel that way, however, just work with the one that feels *the most* right to you.

Why do you think you made this commitment so long ago? What situation or environment might have led you to make this promise to yourself? Close your eyes, and see if any memories come to mind from your childhood when you might have made this commitment. You were probably under the age of 10. If no memories come to you, however, don't worry. It could be that you made the commitment too young for memories. Write whatever comes to mind.

- **Example:** If I'm committed to never rocking the boat, why might that be the case? What am I afraid will happen if I rock the boat? When my parents fought, they got a divorce, which meant I didn't get to see my father very often. That was very painful, and I wanted to avoid feeling that kind of pain ever again.

PART 2: New Commitments and Beliefs

1. Write a new belief and new underlying commitment that declare what you truly want:

- **Example:**

Limiting belief: I believe it's cruel when I say no to my friend's requests, and if I'm cruel, I'm a bad person.

New belief: It's healthy to say no in order to take care of my needs, and I can be a good person even if I say no.

Underlying commitment: I'm committed to living up to my definition of a "good person" because if I don't, I'll feel unworthy.

New commitment: I'm committed to redefining what it means to be a "good person" and knowing that I don't have to earn my worth through my actions.

2. Ask yourself what you'll have to give up in order to make this new commitment.

- **Example:** In order to say no to my friend and set my boundary, I'll have to give up the belief that saying no means I'm a bad person. I'll have to risk upsetting my friend and possibly losing her friendship.

3. Ask yourself what you will gain when you make this new commitment.

- **Example:** If I say no to my friend and set my boundary, I will gain my own self-respect and will take care of myself in the way I deserve. I will no longer feel resentment as a result of doing something I don't want to do. If I lose my friend because of saying no to her, I will discover that she isn't a reasonable friend.

Part 3: Your Inner Child

Take a moment to open your heart and give compassion to your inner child, who created these limiting beliefs and underlying commitments from a place of self-preservation. Honor the child's fear, and make peace with these old commitments. Let your inner child know that you no longer need these old beliefs and commitments and that you're adopting new ones. Affirm that by making these new commitments, you'll be able to set boundaries that will allow you to take better care of your inner child.

I recommend revisiting this exercise periodically because there is little inner work more powerful than determining underlying commitments and creating new commitments. If you find yourself struggling to determine your underlying commitments, however, it might be helpful to work with a coach.

Disowned Qualities

Besides limiting beliefs and underlying commitments, there is another tricky way the psyche keeps us from seeing—and setting—our boundaries. This is by taking certain qualities and disowning them to such a degree that we don't even think we have them. Once again, this pattern was installed when we were very young, when these "disowned qualities" (sometimes called "disowned selves" or "shadow selves") were treated as wrong, problematic, or undesirable by the authority figures in our lives. We had to suppress any "bad" qualities to make sure we were accepted and loved. By hiding them from ourselves, we unconsciously believe we're protecting ourselves from abandonment.

Poet Robert Bly described these disowned qualities as "the long bag we drag behind us." We put all the parts of ourselves we believe we must hide from the world into that bag. "We spend our life until we're twenty deciding what parts of ourself to put in the bag, and we spend the rest of our lives trying to get them out again," he wrote.

Why would we want to get these theoretically terrible qualities back out of the bag? Because if we don't, they reveal themselves in unconscious ways. Yep, I'm talking about that "sideways" thing again. We aren't actually keeping them hidden; it's just that they come out and bite other people when we're not looking! We are also much more prone to seeing these qualities in the people around us. When we cannot "be" these qualities ourselves, we become ultrasensitive to the ways in which others express them openly and without shame.

Disowned qualities are key to the conversation about boundaries because it's our fear of them that keeps us in the people-pleasing, overgiving mode. When we don't set a boundary that we know would benefit us, it's because doing so will make us be something we do *not* want to be. Anytime we feel a strong "yuck" response to being *that*, we can be sure there's a disowned quality hiding nearby.

The truth is that we all possess every human quality and characteristic inside of us, to greater and lesser degrees. We're each kind and cruel, smart and stupid, divine and diabolical. And each quality bears gifts.

When we were babies, we expressed the fullness of our humanity. We cried one minute and laughed the next. We possessed and expressed all qualities and characteristics in a 360-degree personality. But one day, we noticed our parents didn't like certain things we did. They said, "Can't you be still?" or "Don't be so loud!" or "It isn't good to be greedy." To keep our parents' love, we began to reject parts of ourselves—our energetic self, loud self, or greedy self.

As we headed off to school, the chorus of criticism widened to include our caregivers, teachers, friends, and society at large. In trying to make sense of the world, we continued to whittle away at ourselves, rejecting and repressing the parts we deemed unacceptable. As a result, these parts stay hidden in the shadows of our unconscious.

Here's the good news: when you step back into the wholeness of who you are, you're freed from the drive to *not be* something. If you want to set a boundary that sounds selfish to you, you have two opportunities. First, you can bust the myth that setting the boundary is indeed selfish. Second, you can embrace the positive aspect of selfishness that you have been resisting.

Remember when I said that selfishness isn't all bad like we've been taught to believe? If you've decided that taking care of yourself is selfish, embracing what you deem as a little bit of "selfishness" might just be what you need to achieve a healthier balance. It doesn't mean you'll be selfish to the extreme.

Here's another example: one of my main disowned qualities is laziness. I grew up believing that I had to be super efficient in order to be safe, so I overcompensated by trying never to be what I considered lazy. This caused me to become an overachiever. It also made it all the more frustrating that both my ex-husband and my former partner Aaron exhibited behaviors that I previously thought of as lazy.

This is what happens when we disown a part of ourselves—we project that quality outward, and it shows up reflected back to us in other people, much like a mirror. These are the red flags the psyche sends us—the bright neon signs that say, "Look over here to find your disowned qualities!" Seeing—and disdaining—them in others is how we become aware of what needs to be integrated and healed in *ourselves*.

Luckily, by the time I was with Aaron, I had the awareness to see that his so-called laziness boiled down to the fact that he knows how to relax and have fun. When we met, I was in desperate need of some relaxation, and I really believed that fun was for other people. I didn't know the first thing about how to let my hair down and enjoy life. Over the past few years, I've learned by osmosis. I've found my own inner "laziness." In the process I became much more accepting of Aaron's laid-back nature and discovered a version of Nancy who really enjoys a lazy afternoon!

If you're starting to feel scared, don't. Identifying our disowned selves does not—as we often fear—mean we'll become the *worst possible version* of that quality. It's that black-or-white thinking that has kept us wrapped up in judgment about others. I know how to have more fun, but that doesn't mean I've become a couch potato! It simply means I stopped overcompensating for my fear of laziness by working 24/7. As I integrated the laziness inside of me, I began to develop the ability to slow down, stop overworking, and relax more. That's how laziness has a positive aspect to it.

When someone else exhibits a quality that we have disowned, we're usually emotionally triggered by that particular behavior. The trigger can be an indication that we need to dig deep to determine if we're disowning the quality the person is exhibiting. Laziness is a big trigger for me, so I sometimes have to remind myself that I only judge it because it's a disowned quality of mine.

Let me be clear, however: integrating disowned qualities doesn't mean you have to like or accept all behaviors in other people. Each quality can manifest in varying degrees of behavior. I would never want to become overly lazy or selfish, nor would I accept extreme laziness or selfishness in a partner. The shift we are looking to make is to stop going to extremes in the other direction to avoid the disowned quality—including and especially crossing our own boundaries out of fear of being *that*.

If you're struggling to set healthy boundaries, here's a short list of the qualities you may be disowning:

- Self-interest or selfishness
- Anger, rage
- Meanness, cruelty
- Irresponsibility
- Stinginess, lack of generosity
- Being a "taker" not a "giver"

Bear in mind that some qualities we disown may be held as positive ones by others! We may disown our self-confidence because we judge it as a lack of humility. We might disown our intelligence because we think it's elitist. Perhaps we hide our sexiness out of a fear of being seen as "*that* kind of woman," or we keep a lid on our talents for fear of being told we're "showing off."

A good way to find your positive disowned qualities is to think of the people you look up to most. If you admire someone who is brave, for example, it's because you're also brave—it's just in hiding. You aren't expressing it because bravery was, at some point in your past, not a safe thing to be.

Debbie Ford called the integration of these positive qualities "reclaiming our light." She said, "To embrace our light, we understand that we are everything, that we possess every quality. We're not missing anything that we need in order to achieve and fulfill our deepest desires." When we integrate more of our positive qualities and accept our greatness, our capacity for self-love increases and it becomes much easier to set the boundaries we need.

Whatever positive or negative qualities you are currently disowning are already inside of you. It's up to you to become aware of what you've rejected so that you can learn to *appreciate* these qualities and accept them as part of who you are. Consciously integrating these qualities into your personality may be just what you need to set those all-important boundaries you've been unable to set so far.

EXERCISE

Discover Your Disowned Qualities

In this exercise, you'll explore which disowned qualities might be preventing you from setting boundaries. In Part 1, you'll look at negative disowned qualities. In Part 2, you'll do a meditation to help you unearth positive disowned qualities. For the written part of the exercise, write down your answers in a journal or on a device of your choice.

Part 1: Your Negative Disowned Qualities

1. Think about three different people you dislike or feel triggered by. What do you dislike about them? What bothers you about them? Make a list of the qualities that come to mind for each person.

2. Can you think of times in your life when you have exhibited these same qualities? You might have exhibited them differently—and to a less extreme degree—but chances are you have exhibited them in some way, at some time.

3. Ask yourself how you overcompensate to make absolutely sure nobody thinks of you this way. How do you try to manage these qualities and keep them from coming out? For example, if you disown selfishness, you might go out of your way to give to others.

4. Review your Boundary Pyramid, and choose the boundary you want to set the most—perhaps the one you are the most scared to set. Have you judged yourself for wanting to set this boundary? What do you fear others might say about you if you do set it? Would they say you're mean or irresponsible? Would they say you're selfish or "a taker"? Using your answers in this exercise as clues, write down what you believe are the disowned qualities you are afraid you'd "be" if you set this scary boundary.

5. Now write down a positive aspect of each disowned quality. For example, if the quality is

selfishness, the positive aspect might be sticking up for yourself, taking your share, or embracing self-care. If the quality is irresponsibility, the positive aspect could be spontaneity or fun. If the quality is laziness, the positive aspect could be the ability to relax.

6. Lastly, choose one action that you can take this week to begin to integrate one of these positive aspects into your life. For example, if your disowned quality is selfishness, choose one action this week that you would judge as selfish. It might be as simple as taking an hour to spend exactly as you want with no interruptions.

Part 2: Your Positive Disowned Qualities

Now let's turn our attention to positive disowned qualities. This part of the exercise will be a short meditation. For this portion, be sure to turn off all phones so that you can surrender to the process. Wear unrestricting clothes, and sit in a comfortable chair or couch. Feel free to play soft music or light candles, if you like. It helps to record your own voice reading the steps so that you don't have to open your eyes, which will disrupt your meditative state. (You may wish to skip the italicized portions of the meditation in your recording.)

1. Close your eyes, and take several deep breaths. Relax each part of your body, starting with your feet. Then gradually move up your legs, hips, belly, chest, back, arms, neck, and head until you feel fully relaxed. *Don't work too hard at this. Just*

ask your body to relax. As you continue, it will relax more and more.

2. Imagine that someone else (it could be someone you know or an imaginary person) is setting the boundary you most want to set. This person finds it easy to set this boundary. As you observe them setting it, ask yourself what quality they have that allows them to set this boundary with ease. Are they courageous? Do they have a high level of self-respect? Are they strong and powerful?

3. Can you recall a time in your past when you displayed this positive quality? If so, picture yourself at that time. What were you doing? How did you feel?

4. Ask yourself when you decided it was no longer safe to express this quality. What happened to make you disown it?

5. Who in your life today exhibits this quality without shame or embarrassment? These are the people you have projected the quality onto. Do you admire them for it?

6. Affirm to yourself that you're ready to reclaim this quality so that it can support you in setting your boundaries.

7. What belief would you have to give up in order to integrate this quality and exhibit it in your life?

8. Imagine yourself letting go of this belief and fully integrating this positive quality. Then

imagine yourself setting the boundary with the same ease as the other person you visualized. How does it feel to have this quality available to you and set the boundary you most want to set?

9. Identify one action you can take this week to begin to integrate this quality into your life. If the quality is courage, what small thing can you do this week that's courageous? Each week, choose another action that's more courageous, building up your ability to integrate and express this quality in your life.

Excuses, Excuses

Besides our underlying commitments and disowned qualities, it's important to unearth and name our go-to excuses for not setting the boundaries we most need. In fact, these excuses often help us pinpoint our underlying commitments and disowned qualities.

Excuses can be very sneaky, sounding so logical and definitive that we convince ourselves they are *absolutely true* and we *can't possibly set the boundaries* we most need to set. But just like limiting beliefs, our excuses are not facts. They, too, are based in fear. Their logic is the result of a warped view of the world and is not trustworthy. Their sole purpose is to prevent us from doing something we believe will put us in some kind of danger—for our purposes, the "something" is setting a boundary.

Excuses are how we hold our resistance in place. Debbie Ford defined *resistance* as "an unconscious protective defense mechanism, a programmed reaction rather than a conscious choice." Out of our fear, we resist what's good for us—i.e., setting the boundaries we need for our own well-being.

Excuses are often phrased as "I could never . . . " or "I don't know how to. . . . " Using "I could never" allows us to pretend we have no choice in the matter. What we actually mean by "I could never" is "I *would* never." And when we say, "I don't know how," what we mean is that "I don't know how . . . yet." We can always learn.

The point is that most of the time, we *can* set even the scariest boundary—if only we're *willing* to step past our resistance. Giving in to our excuses is a choice we make.

Try replacing your "I can't set the boundary of _____" with "I'm resistant to setting the boundary of _____." For example, change "I can't set the boundary of leaving when my husband drinks too much" to "I'm resistant to setting the boundary of leaving when my husband drinks too much." Do you see how different the second sentence feels? It leaves the door of possibility open.

Here's an example. Natalia believed she had to be accepted by others in order to be safe. She bent over backward to cross her own boundaries and make sure everyone else was pleased with her. This led to excuses to like, "I can't tell my best friend I don't want to travel with her because it will hurt her feelings," and "I don't know how to raise my rates without losing clients."

Other common excuses to avoid setting boundaries include: "I'll do it tomorrow when I'm not so tired," "I'll talk to her later in the week, when she isn't under so much stress," and "I'll set the boundary the *next* time she crosses it."

Our excuses are a type of self-sabotage that give us permission not to set important boundaries. We rationalize our choices in order to stay in our comfort zone. That makes sense to the child within, but for the adult, it keeps us locked in self-destructive patterns.

Clients sometimes insist that the roadblocks *are not excuses, they're facts.* So, how can you tell an excuse from an actual fact? An excuse is usually about the future, while a fact is about the present. Let's say you and your boss don't get along, and trying to navigate that relationship day after day is draining you. The boundary you need to set is that you will not work for that person anymore. A fact might be, "I can't afford to quit my job because I have no savings." Having a zero balance in your savings is indeed a fact. And it's true that quitting your job without knowing where your next paycheck is coming from is a terrible idea. But of course, leaving your job right now isn't the only option. You can take action steps today to look for another job, while keeping the one you have in the meantime. It's important not to hide behind the facts, using them to keep yourself stuck.

An example of an excuse rather than a fact might be: "I can't look for another job because no one would hire me at my age." That's a projection about the future, based on a *belief* about age. While your age might make finding another job more complex, it doesn't mean you *can't* find one. Again, excuses like these serve to keep us in familiar territory—falsely limiting the possibilities that are available to us.

Debbie Ford suggested that we make our lives an "excuse-free zone." When we want or need something, we either take responsibility for not having it ("Looking for another job sounds uncomfortable, so I'm going to stay where I am"), or we take steps to get the thing we want ("I'm afraid no one will hire me at my age, but I'm going to send out résumés anyway"). The next time you catch yourself using an excuse for not setting a boundary, stop yourself. Reread this chapter (Step 4), and start the process of setting the boundary you need in order to be happy and well.

The "What If?" Syndrome

Since our limiting beliefs, underlying commitments, and excuses are always based in fear, they're no more real than the monster we believed was in the closet when we were kids. These fears breed what I call the *"What if?"* syndrome—keeping us locked in worst-case scenarios and preventing us from setting healthy boundaries.

Here are some common "what if" excuses:

- What if I tell my husband how I feel, and he leaves me?

- What if I ask my boss for time off, and she fires me?

- What if I refuse to give my son money, and he's mad at me?

There are an endless number of "what if" possibilities, driving us crazy with doom and gloom stories. Most of these scenarios are unlikely to happen, but we still use them to fuel our excuses and avoid the boundaries we're afraid to set.

EXERCISE

Take Stock of Your Excuses

In this exercise, you will write down some of your go-to excuses and evaluate how real they actually are.

1. Choose three important boundaries from your Boundary Pyramid. Write down the excuses you use for not setting each boundary. For example:

- *Excuse:* "I can't tell my daughter she has to move out of the house because then she'll end up on the street."

2. Is this excuse definitively true? Are you sure? In the example, it's clearly not the only possible outcome. It's simply the worst possible outcome you can imagine. It's your belief, but not a fact, that your daughter will end up on the street. There are other options, no? She might go live with her dad. She might go live with a friend. She might get a job and be able to pay her own rent. Make a list of at least three other possible outcomes—however unlikely they seem to you—from setting the boundary you've chosen.

3. Now rephrase each of the excuses as resistance/belief, and write the new phrases.

- *Sample rephrased excuse:* "I'm *resistant to* telling my daughter she has to move out of the house because I *believe* she will end up on the street."

For now, you don't need to set the boundary. Just knowing your excuses is a big step. As you continue through the steps of the book, you will begin to release your resistance more and more as you learn new strategies for setting boundaries.

With all of this unconscious material in the way, it's no wonder we're so uncomfortable with setting boundaries. So one of the key steps to becoming a boundary badass is learning to *get comfortable with discomfort*—which is precisely the next step on our journey.

REMEMBER

When you unearth your underlying commitments, disowned qualities, and excuses, you make it possible to set healthy boundaries.

GET COMFORTABLE WITH
SHORT-TERM DISCOMFORT

Jessica and her sister Kate have spent more than a year closing their mother's estate, which involves managing the motel their mom owned. "I've gone along with what Kate wants," Jessica says, "deciding I'd rather have a relationship than a fight." Kate has made it clear she wants to maintain the hotel, and Jessica knows her sister has no money to buy out Jessica's share. "I've played a role as the agreeable sister," Jessica says, "not telling Kate that I want to sell the motel and be done with it. I've basically lied to her, presenting a false persona, while hoping I could convince myself I wasn't upset and continue to sacrifice my best interests. Recently, a favorite relative refused to get off the phone with me until I wrote the e-mail to Kate that I'd wanted to write for a year, saying that we should either sell the motel or find a way for her to pay me what I'm owed for my portion. I apologized for my change of heart because it isn't cool. But it also isn't cool to continue supplanting my needs for my sister."

After all of Jessica's worries about the situation, her sister's response was simply, "That sounds good."

Often, we avoid boundaries because we assume the worst is going to happen. We believe we'll start a war with the other people involved. That we'll lose relationships. That we'll end up feeling like a terrible or—God forbid—*selfish* person. Our fears skip right to the extreme, and we think in black-and-white, all-or-nothing terms. We believe we either have to completely deny ourselves or face horrible consequences with others.

While there can indeed be consequences to setting boundaries, many of my clients, like Jessica, have discovered that the results haven't been as extreme as they anticipated. As Jessica puts it: "I realized that speaking (or writing, in this case) clearly and reasonably sometimes *does* work, and it's such an energy suck and waste of time to assume the worst. My approach in the past has contributed to my being seen as someone who will back down. But when I decided I deserved to be treated fairly, I was able to uphold my boundary."

Tina set the boundary of stepping away from doing "mom" things when her husband is at home. Recently, she left her daughter at home with a friend from school for a playdate and relied on her husband to take care of the situation.

"The old me said, 'I can't leave during a playdate, especially since it's the first time this friend has been to our home. That would be rude, selfish, and disconnected.' But the truth is I'm already disconnected—from myself. So I left. This is the beginning of what feels like a bigger boundary, and I know I'm on to something because my eyes are welling with tears as I write this. I know it has nothing to do with leaving a playdate. It's bigger," she says.

Tina has endured the long-term suffering of feeling disconnected from herself in order to avoid the short-term discomfort of asking her husband to take some responsibility for their daughter's care. Jessica endured the long-term suffering of helping to manage the motel when she didn't have the time or energy for it. Plus, she could have used the money from the sale of her portion. She did all that to avoid the short-term discomfort of potential conflict with her sister.

No matter which choice we make, there's going to be some discomfort. But choosing not to set the boundary we need prolongs that discomfort indefinitely. Setting the boundary is "the discomfort that ends the discomfort." Bonus: It builds our muscle of self-love and self-respect in the process.

So Step 5 is *Get Comfortable with Short-Term Discomfort.*

The Power of Discomfort

What would life be like if we weren't running from discomfort all the time? We'd get used to momentary uneasiness because we would learn how to work with it when it presents itself. We'd resolve any issues quickly. Our energy wouldn't be constantly drained from trying to avoid our own feelings, the feelings of others, and the terror of rocking the boat.

Why do we avoid short-term discomfort so much? It has to do with our natural human tendency to keep uncertainty at bay. *What if the worst happens?* (There's that old "what if" syndrome again.) So we opt for a *familiar* discomfort rather than an *unfamiliar* one. We know we can survive our own suffering; we've come this far, anyway! But we don't know if we can survive the reactions of others. Staying in our suffering is a hefty price to pay for certainty, but at least we think we know how it's going to turn out.

My client Judy says she stayed in a bad relationship for more than six years to avoid the short-term discomfort of breaking up and moving out. She was afraid he would be hurt, and she would feel unbearable guilt as a result. She worried that she would feel lonely and struggle to find a new relationship. When she finally did it, however, she wondered why she had waited so long. Her boyfriend was hurt, but he got over it and went on with his life. She felt lonely for a short period of time but ultimately felt much happier outside of the unhealthy relationship. If she had given herself permission to leave when she felt the need, she could have experienced that happiness six years earlier.

My client Paula has realized that not setting boundaries can cause problems not just for her, but for others as well. "I had a situation in which one of the co-leaders of my meditation group allowed someone into the group who didn't fit the criteria we had all agreed upon. He admitted that he let the person into the group in order to avoid making waves. He then said he would tell the new participant they had to leave, but before he could do it, he tried to push it off on me. I proudly handed the task back to him." It was interesting for Paula to observe someone else choosing long-term discomfort over the temporary pain of conflict—something she might have done in a previous time. Letting the participant attend had created a lot more "waves" than saying no from the start would have. "That example helped me see the impact on other people when we don't set our boundaries. I have compassion for him about it, but I'm also not stepping in to fix it for him," she says.

Here's a hypothetical example: If your wife tells you regularly that you're fat, you might say nothing even though it hurts your feelings. After all, you've already tolerated her verbal abuse for a long time. You know how to do that because it's a familiar pain, and you've built up a tolerance to that pain over time by numbing your feelings.

You actually don't know what will happen if you ask for her to stop commenting on your waistline; you've never tried it. But you jump to your worst possible fear that if you said something to her, it might cause an argument or, worse yet, end your relationship. Even though the constant abuse is awful and causes you significant and regular pain, you swallow your feelings to avoid the uncertainty of her response. In the process, you deprive yourself of what you deserve: the feeling of being respected and treated kindly by your partner.

This dance we do not only pits long-term discomfort against short-term discomfort, but also *internal* discomfort against *external* discomfort. We opt for the *internal* discomfort of facing our own suffering rather than risk the *external* discomfort of possible conflict. Of course, we're feeling discomfort either way—and only one of the options on the menu has the potential to end the discomfort once and for all.

When we were children, conflict with our loved ones was legitimately too much for us to handle. Our little nervous systems couldn't tolerate the possibility that we might be exiled or abandoned, because we relied so heavily on our authority figures to keep us alive. But as adults, we *can* survive. Conflict might be uncomfortable, but it's survivable. And the reward we receive for walking through (usually temporary) conflict with someone else is a lifetime of freedom—the opportunity to live the life of our own making.

Soon, we're going to explore what that life of freedom might look like for you. But take it from someone who avoided conflict to her own detriment for decades—life on your own terms is well worth any discomfort it might take to get there.

The willingness to feel the short-term
discomfort of setting boundaries
is the gateway to everything you've
ever wanted in your life.

We simply cannot create a life we love without setting boundaries. It isn't possible. Yes, there is risk involved. But when we drill down, we see that what we're most afraid of is that we might *feel* something we don't want to feel. We are keeping ourselves stuck in patterns that don't serve us because we're afraid of what we will have to feel if we don't. In other words, we're being held hostage by our own *emotions*. (Yes, our *own* emotions—not the emotions of others. The only thing that makes us afraid others will have feelings is our belief that we won't survive what *we* will have to feel in response. It's ultimately about us, not them.)

What's the antidote? Getting familiar with discomfort—which boils down to negative emotions—so we learn it's not going to kill us. The more willing we are to feel the guilt, shame, and sadness we've been avoiding, the less power those emotions have over us. It's only through avoidance and procrastination that we give these emotions so much power. Emotions are like the weather; they come and go. They don't last forever. But somehow we've become convinced that they are so dangerous we must do everything we can to avoid having them.

Let's say a friend tells you that you *should* join her at an expensive retreat that you don't want to attend. In the past, you would have agreed to go in order to avoid the short-term internal discomfort of hurting her feelings and the possible external discomfort of an argument. You would have attended a retreat you couldn't afford and felt resentful toward your friend because of it.

But after working on your boundary badassery, you catch yourself and say, "It sounds like a great retreat for you, but it isn't something I want to do." Even if your friend continues to try to talk you into it, you stick to your decision and say, "I'm not interested in the retreat, and I'd like to stop talking about it now. Let's discuss what we can plan that we'd both enjoy doing together."

Yes, it's uncomfortable, especially for a people pleaser, to turn down the retreat that your friend wants so much for you to attend. But once you've made your feelings clear, it will likely be over. Your fear that it would ruin the relationship is proven unfounded, and any whiffs of guilt or shame quickly pass. Resentment, on the other hand, sticks around. You may sweep it under the rug, but you can be sure it will still be there when you dare to peek again. The number-one problem I see in my clients' most important relationships is a buildup of unspoken, unprocessed resentment. It is the most common wedge that divides couples and ends friendships.

While it's possible that your friend will be upset that you don't want to attend the retreat, it's much more likely that your friendship will suffer from the long-term resentment you would feel if you crossed your boundary. And let's face it—if your friend can't honor your decision to skip the retreat, this may be a friendship to reconsider.

In order to slay the dragon of our short-term discomfort, we have to be willing to feel our emotions. We have to stop avoiding our feelings and trying to ignore them. Feeling them in the moment is the key to freedom. But that freedom requires that we stop putting aside who we are, what we feel, what we want, and what we need.

Cozying Up to Conflict

The freedom we want also requires what I call "cozying up to conflict." I wrote about this extensively in *Permission to Put Yourself First*. As I've said, long-term resentment is much more damaging to our relationships than short-term conflict. But because we're raised to believe that relationships are supposed to be harmonious at all costs, we often run from even the smallest of issues. In fact, we believe that something is wrong when a relationship isn't always easy.

But consistent harmony in any relationship is unrealistic. Conflict will occur between people no matter how hard we try to avoid it. And the longer we avoid it, the more the resentment festers. My client Margaret has avoided the short-term discomfort of a conversation with her husband about her sensual and intimate desires. She fears that he won't understand and will become upset, so she puts off discussing it with him. As a result, she feels more and more disconnected from him, putting the relationship in real jeopardy.

Instead of seeing it as dangerous, we must reframe conflict as an opportunity to grow. *Differences don't have to be a problem; they can be functional.* They can be a portal to evolving the relationship into something even better and more whole. Conflict doesn't have to mean that one person "wins" or is "right," while another person "loses" or is "wrong." We can cohabitate without agreeing on everything. Remember, connection is more important than consensus.

While not everyone we encounter will see conflict in a positive way, the price we pay for placating others' fear is our own long-term comfort. The more we're able to withstand conflict and see it as simply part of a healthy relationship rather than a flaw, the more we're able to set boundaries that help us sustain our relationships in a healthy way.

Harmony at all costs in our relationships creates disharmony inside ourselves. Inner harmony *requires* that we set boundaries. When we don't fully engage in external conflict, we deal with internal conflict on a regular, long-term basis. The dance of internal versus external conflict is similar to the dance of internal versus external discomfort.

My client Elaine puts it this way: "It's always the trepidation of confrontation that has me rationalizing why it's okay to reconsider setting a boundary. I call it compassion and understanding for others, but I end up forgetting that I deserve compassion and understanding too."

Essentially, boundary badassery means you stop accepting long-term discomfort to avoid short-term discomfort—full stop. You set a boundary as soon as you notice you have a need or a want. You come to expect and anticipate the short-term discomfort, and you learn that it isn't going to kill you. You never, ever opt for long-term discomfort again. In some very real way, the entire process in this book is my way of supporting you to do this one thing: brave the discomfort of possible conflict, proving to yourself that it won't kill you.

EXERCISE

Where Have You Been Conflict-Averse?

In this exercise, you'll explore the relationships in your life in which you have avoided conflict. Write your answers down in a journal or on a device of your choice.

1. Write down every relationship in your life in which you struggle to keep the peace.

2. For each one, consider which boundaries you have to ignore in order to maintain the relationship, and write them down.

- **Example:** *I struggle to keep the peace with my husband's older brother. I have to cross my boundary of hearing inappropriate stories about his sexual exploits whenever he calls me to talk.*

3. How does crossing these boundaries make you feel? What is the long-term discomfort you've endured as a result of not setting these boundaries?

- **Example:** *I hate talking to my brother-in-law, and he has no idea how I feel. I'm uncomfortable keeping my feelings from him, and I'm uncomfortable hearing his stories, which make my skin crawl. I endure the discomfort whenever our family gets together, as well as the discomfort of keeping my feelings from my husband.*

4. If you have discovered any new boundaries that need setting as a result of this exercise, add them in the appropriate layer on your Boundary Pyramid.

Your Comfort Zone

We all have an arbitrary comfort zone that we've created in our minds based on our past. Whenever we experience trauma, we make a mental note (often unconscious) to avoid ever going through *that* again. So we set up barriers that create our comfort zone, and we fear going beyond those barriers. For all we know, it would lead to the same trauma we experienced previously. But since this comfort zone is based on past experiences, it has nothing to do with our current reality. Often, we create it when we're children and never move beyond it, even though we're much stronger as adults and able to withstand the challenges that setting a boundary might create.

Most of us actually have a much more expansive comfort zone than we think. We can tolerate more short-term discomfort than we expect—especially if we keep in mind how much less suffering it means in the long term.

There's a saying that goes, "Life begins at the end of your comfort zone." The next time you feel afraid to take a step in a new direction, especially one you fear others will be surprised or upset by, remember this saying. Staying comfortable has its benefits, but it comes at the expense of aliveness. If you've shielded yourself from conflict since you were very small, consider giving it another try as an adult. If being in "giving" mode is way easier for you than asking for help, for instance, test-drive making a small ask of someone you know who loves and supports you. These baby steps will let you sample life outside of your current comfort zone—and very likely, will expand your ability to be comfortable in a much wider variety of situations.

The Dreaded Consequences

While I've witnessed my clients set new, scary boundaries and experience none of the awful consequences they anticipated, that isn't always the case. There will certainly be times when setting a boundary results in real consequences that can be quite painful. You may find that you have to sacrifice certain relationships or enter into difficult conflicts with people in your life. The person on the other side of your boundary may or may not uphold, respect, agree, or validate it.

But remember that there are also very real consequences associated with *not* setting boundaries. In each circumstance, only you can decide which set of consequences is more important. Remember, it's your choice. You get to determine your priorities. For each situation, you must ask yourself: *What's my top priority here, and does a boundary need to be set in order for that top priority to be met?* (Of course, if you find that avoidance of conflict is still your top priority, go back and revisit Steps 1 through 3!)

If you think setting a boundary will lead to the loss of any close relationship, you have to ask yourself what's most important to you. How far are you willing to go—or not go? What are you willing to endure in order to keep this person in your life? Is the most important thing to maintain the relationship or to honor your boundary? Only you can know.

My client Zoe and her family eventually ended their relationship with her mother-in-law. "We allowed her to be mean and judgmental and chalked it up to age, but it was constant and created a lot of resentment and rage for me. Finally, we told her we would not allow our daughter to be around that behavior and spelled out what we meant. She told us we coddled our daughter too much (even though she was only three years old) and immediately went back to her normal, mean behavior, telling us what she thought we were doing wrong with our lives. We no longer have any relationship with her, and it has been a very heavy weight lifted. Even though it goes against my Pollyanna need to be liked and to like everyone, it was the healthiest thing for our family."

For years, my friend Carla walked on eggshells around her father to try to avoid sending him into one of his infamous rages. Two Christmases in a row, she endured all-day rages from him when she visited her parents for the holidays. In the past, she felt she had to visit them since it was one of the few times during the year when she got to see them. But finally, she'd had enough. She wrote her father a letter telling him exactly how she felt and explained why she would not spend Christmas with them the following year.

The letter, of course, sent her father into another rage, and Carla's mother was around to hear it. She called Carla, begging her daughter to apologize. "Mom," Carla said, "I would do just about anything for you, but he's the one who owes me an apology. Asking me to apologize to him is asking me to be untrue to myself, and that's one of the few things I can't do for you. I love you, but I won't say I'm sorry for telling the truth and taking care of myself."

Setting this boundary was painful for Carla. She didn't want her mother to have to listen to her father's rage, and she wanted to be able to spend time with both her parents over the holidays. But it was empowering for her to finally take care of herself, doing what she needed for her own well-being and expressing her truth to her father, regardless of the consequences. The pain was short-term compared to the long-term suffering of always swallowing her feelings and doing the bidding of her father's unreasonable demands. As my client Bob puts it, "The comfort of being true to myself is far better than the comfort of calming the waters for someone else."

Laura went through a difficult situation with her aunt and uncle, who bought property next to hers. Even though she asked them not to buy horses, they did it anyway and just assumed that Laura and her family would care for the animals. Her aunt paid them for the horses' care, but it was a lot of extra work for them that they didn't want to do. Then, her aunt expected them to do more and more.

"Every time I said yes to her requests," Laura says, "I felt a knot in my stomach. I had trouble sleeping at night and became depressed because I felt so trapped. We even looked at other properties where we could move, but we wanted to stay on our property."

When Laura protested about the arrangement, her aunt threatened financial repercussions. "It took four years before I finally set a boundary with them that stuck," Laura says. "I got to the point where I told them to go ahead and sue us. We would countersue. They never did. It was one of the hardest things I've ever done in my life and one that empowered me beyond anything I'd done previously. While we no longer have a relationship with them, it was absolutely necessary to set that boundary."

Some boundary-setting situations will be explosive, no matter how you handle them. But you may also be surprised with the positive changes that happen in your relationships when you set boundaries. When you connect with your truth and change the way you show up in relationships, it gives other people permission to do the same.

That's what happened for Candace, who experienced some consequences when she set a boundary with her sister.

"I let her know that I was unavailable for negativity-filled communication or requests for money," Candace says. "I had a terrible pinched nerve in my left shoulder, and the pain wouldn't subside until I set this boundary. My sister's response was to respect my boundary, but she deleted me from Facebook." They had little communication for a couple of months, but then, her sister expressed a desire to reconcile. Candace has maintained her boundary with her sister, and the relationship has been much smoother.

Nevertheless, we have real fears when we get ready to set boundaries, especially the big ones with people we love. So in the exercise that follows this section, I'm going to invite you to "catastrophize" the consequences you're most afraid of. What terrible, awful, earth-shattering cost might you have to pay if you set one of your biggest boundaries? This may not sound like a particularly fun exercise, but naming the worst-case scenario is like shining a light under the bed to see the monster you've been afraid of. Only once you've looked directly at it can you make an informed decision.

Often, I find my clients are *sure* something devastating will happen if they take this step, but when they go looking for what, exactly, they're afraid of, all they can find is a feeling of "very, very bad." This is the case because, as I've said before, our worst fears were formed in childhood—often before we had the language to truly describe them. And as I mentioned earlier, the fear is actually just the fear of a *feeling*—a very, very bad feeling. But once we look at this feeling with the eyes of an adult, we discover it's actually tolerable. Moreover, it's rare in my experience that the worst-case scenario actually turns out to be true.

My client Renee's worst fear is defamation and exposure on social media. "A boundary I can't seem to set is breaking off communication with my ex-girlfriend. I fear her doing a Facebook smear campaign and defaming me. I fear her anger. I also fear losing her friendship. I fear the rejection. I feel I would be a horrible person for having brought my dog, myself, and my children into her life, and then having taken it all away."

I could relate to what Renee was feeling. Exposure was also my greatest fear for a long time, and it was exactly the button my ex-husband pushed when he read my journals and threatened to send certain pages to the most important people in my life. While that threat never panned out, he did indeed defame me on Facebook. I'm not going to say it was pleasant, but it certainly didn't kill me. And it blew over without major consequences because the people who are truly important in my life knew better than to believe what he said. Despite that defamation, I now have a successful career as a coach and author. I know this kind of exposure can be explosive in some situations, so I'm not making light of the potential repercussions. But as we become more aware of the consequences we fear, we can see them from a more rational place and act accordingly. Are they truly likely to happen?

So let's do some "catastrophizing" right now, with one or two of your most dreaded boundaries, and see what we come up with.

EXERCISE

Create Your Dreaded List of Consequences (DLC)

Revisit your Boundary Pyramid, and choose one or two boundaries that you feel you absolutely cannot set! Then, follow these steps for each boundary you choose. Write down your answers in a journal or on the device of your choice.

1. Write down the boundary, and below it list all the reasons why you absolutely *cannot* set it.

2. Name all of the horrible outcomes that you're *sure* will happen if you set the boundary. What is the worst-case "what if" scenario?

3. Who in your life will this boundary be hardest on?

4. What kind of horrible person would you be if you set this boundary? Would you be cruel? Selfish? Unreasonable? Unloving? Write down everything you're afraid to be.

5. Now, let's switch gears. What would be the *benefits* of setting this boundary? How will your life change for the better when this boundary is in place?

6. Think of someone who loves and supports you completely, someone who would be a champion for you setting this boundary. (If you can't find someone you know personally, use me!) Imagine this person giving you a pep talk, laying out at least four specific reasons you are worthy of setting this boundary. Examples might include:

- *Individuals are entitled to care for themselves* at least *as much as they care for others, and this includes you!*

- *You are worthy of comfort, self-love, and self-respect!*

- *You deserve better than having to delete your own needs and desires in service of others!*

Don't worry, I'm not going to ask you to set any of these most difficult boundaries . . . *yet*. But I think you *are* ready to do some really important prep work toward that outcome: imagining what your life will be like when you become the boundary badass you're meant to be—and (shiver) what it would have been like if you *hadn't* decided to do the boundary work in this book. Both scenarios are equally informative, in different ways. Let's dive in!

REMEMBER

The willingness to feel the short-term discomfort of setting boundaries is the gateway to everything you've ever wanted in your life.

ENVISION YOUR EMPOWERED FUTURE

"My husband cheated on me. When we talked things through, he said he would stay with me for our son," Paula says. "I said that wasn't good enough for me. I wanted someone to stay with me because they wanted to *be* with me." It was clear to Paula that her future would be bleak if she stayed in a loveless marriage, so she gathered the courage to set the boundary that she would not stay under those circumstances.

As expected, Paula's choice had consequences. "I became a single mom, my income was reduced, and we had to move to a more cost-effective home," she recalls. But the benefits ultimately outweighed the consequences. "I also became debt-free and started to find myself after losing myself in my marriage. I started having more fun. I even gained some free time on the weekends when my son went to be with his dad."

When she completes her journey toward boundary badassery, Paula imagines her life will be a lot freer, more open, and less restrictive. "I will feel like I can do what I want, when I want, without even having thoughts of the opinions of others. I will fully let go of doing things out of a sense of obligation. I will speak up right away when something feels off, instead of waiting until I can't stand it anymore. I will shift the energy immediately, instead of stewing on it," she says.

While going through the 10-step process in this book, Jessica realized something funny: She can't decide what to order at a restaurant without first checking what the other person is going to order. Then she orders the same thing because she believes this makes her more likeable and more pleasing as a companion. "Not letting the opinions or feelings of others affect me would mean giving up people-pleasing," Jessica says, "which would be a huge, wonderful shift. If I set boundaries, I might finally figure out who I am, what I like, be treated with more respect by others, have more positive people in my life, and feel happier about my life in general. My life will quite possibly look unrecognizable from the life I'm living today."

Often, we fail to see the *positive* possibilities on the other side of setting a boundary. First, we're so afraid of the worst-case scenario that it's all we can imagine. Second, the positive outcomes are often unfamiliar and thus difficult to envision. This was completely true for me. Even though my marriage was a mess, I went back to my husband several times before I finally had the courage to end it. I didn't have the capacity to see how truly happy and free my life could become without that relationship. My marriage was all I could envision for myself.

Several years ago, I was on a hike with my bestie, Kelly. She was trying to help me see all the possibilities that lay beyond the constraints I was feeling in the present— daring me to imagine even *one single possible scenario* of what my life could be like five years down the line. The more she tried to get me to name possibilities, the more constricted, shut down, and tearful I became. I didn't know why I felt so triggered; it was just a silly exercise! But the thought of imagining anything better for myself than what I had at that moment was nearly impossible for me at that time.

Looking back on it, I wish I could have gotten even the tiniest glimpse of the life I have now. There is no comparing my former life with my current one. I'm not saying everything is always sunshine and roses, but I live my life on my own terms today. I have an entrepreneurial career I love, a lively and honest relationship, and the freedom to make choices I never knew I had before. I don't worry so much about what others think of me, and I put myself first. This has made all the difference.

As hard as it can be (and I know from personal experience that it can be super triggering!) it's critically important to build the muscle of imagination. That glimpse, or even just a whiff, of what's possible on the other side is the fuel we need in order to set the boundaries we most need to set. When we're able to envision a new life, we're much more likely to take the necessary action to see it through. That vision is what gives us the confidence and courage to make better choices for ourselves.

Now, let me be clear. I'm not saying you need to pull out the glue sticks and magazines to create a vision board. While you can certainly create one if that's your thing, I personally haven't created a vision board in more than two decades. (Shocking for a Hay House author, I know!) As it happens, I'm not a fan of magical thinking—or even the Law of Attraction. I don't believe they work as stand-alone techniques. In my view, positive action is required to create the life we most want. And the first act we each must take is changing the deeply held belief that setting boundaries is dangerous and impossible.

As I look back on what I went through in ending my marriage and disclosing my true self to my family, friends, and co-workers, I can also imagine what my life would have been like if I had *not* split up with my husband. I would, no doubt, still be with him, hiding from the aspects of myself that I deemed unacceptable. I would never have become a coach or written a single book, let alone several. I wouldn't have a weekly radio show with Hay House, and I wouldn't have the honor of helping so many people improve the quality of their lives. It's so sad for me to think that all of this might never have happened.

Of course, setting boundaries doesn't mean you have to end a relationship—that was just my story. But it's still a good idea to look at the potential outcomes, both positive and negative, as you're preparing to set certain boundaries. That way, you can make a wise choice to either set the boundary or not—from a place of courage rather than fear.

So Step 6 is about envisioning what your future will be like in both scenarios. First, the future you'll have if you decide the consequences are too painful to set certain boundaries. Then, the future you'll have if you decide the time has come to set them, whatever the outcome. Either scenario is totally valid, I want to be clear about that. Especially if you're working with one of the boundaries in the good-to-have layer of your pyramid, it's often the most valid choice to say okay to not setting one of those boundaries if the consequences would outweigh the desire.

For example, let's say you and your partner have different vacation styles. You're not a beach person, but your husband could live in a cabana. You want to set a boundary: no more beach vacations. But the impact on your husband would be great, since he grew up by the ocean and needs to get his "fix" at least once a year. Are you going to give up all the wonderful things about him, leaving the relationship, just because you can't drink one more piña colada? Probably not. And that's a totally valid choice.

This step—*Envision Your Empowered Future*—will be a bit more exercise-heavy than the others, but if you make the commitment to do the work, I promise it will be one of the most enlightening steps in the process.

Boundaries and Desire

Before we work on your respective visions of the future, we need to take a moment to talk about desire. Boundaries and desire are closely interrelated. Only once we shed light on what we want—and specifically, what we're *not* getting that we desire—can we really begin to know which boundaries we need to set. I would go so far as to say that setting boundaries is the number-one most effective action we can take on the road to a life where we get more and more of what we want.

The concept of "creating a life based on what we want" can be confusing at first. Most of us have spent our lives blaming fate—or other people—for the fact that we don't have what we want most. We imagine that others need to act or behave in particular ways in order for us to be happy, and we ourselves have neither the responsibility nor the blame when we're disappointed by our lives. We don't notice that a big part of why we haven't gotten what we want is our own failure to ask for it—in large part by setting boundaries.

I'm not suggesting you blame yourself, nor am I ignoring the very real advantages and disadvantages that various groups of people experience in the world. It's true that some of us have more of an uphill battle in creating what we want than others, and it's one of the great works of our lifetimes to demand an equal playing field for all human beings, regardless of race, gender, sexual orientation, or religion.

At the same time, being part of a traditionally oppressed group does not mean we have no agency in our lives at all. If you are reading this book, it's because you're ready to claim the responsibility you *do* have for the choices you've made. Positive changes stand on the other side of the decision to take personal responsibility for our lives, even as we still have much work to do toward ending systemic racism, sexism, and gender discrimination in the big picture.

I want you to feel empowered to make changes for yourself because I've seen people in all kinds of circumstances turn their lives around for the better. And those changes happened because they (1) believed change was possible for them, and (2) took determined action to make it happen.

The initial step, however, is to figure out what we want in the first place! For some of us, this isn't clear at all. We've spent so many years putting our own desires aside in order to take care of everyone else that we may not even know what we want.

When my client Gabrielle began to explore what she wanted in her life that she wasn't getting, she realized she wanted to alter her financial situation. Specifically, she wanted to revise some agreements she'd made to her children with regard to money.

"For example," she says, "I co-signed a car for my son. Even though I've bailed him out on payments twice, he's still behind. I've told him that I won't cover it anymore. While this is a positive boundary, the result is that every month it's behind, it's a negative mark on my credit."

What would Gabrielle like instead? "When it comes to the car payments, I want my son to become more financially responsible and keep up the payments. In the bigger picture, I want more money and more freedom to travel," she says. "I also want to change my job situation, which is continuing to suck the life out of me. So I need to rethink what more money and freedom would look like, and set boundaries to achieve that."

If you aren't getting what you want out of your life, setting boundaries has the potential to be a game changer for you. My client Megan reflects, "It feels like I'm not getting what I want in most areas of my life. I recently realized I'm living the life everyone else desired for me. Given that I didn't even know about boundaries, I think they're related to everything. I don't have financial independence or a career that engages or supports me. I went along with what my husband and our accountant wanted—decisions that best suited his business rather than my quality of life. Part of it is due to not realizing how much my parents were forcing their worldview on me from their idea of families and women's roles, to their religion, to their politics. My marriage has had many good moments, but there has been an underlying thread of disrespect toward me from both my husband and his parents. I sat here and took it all, never set boundaries and never had the self-confidence or self-esteem to think I could uphold them or survive on my own." How long can she go on like this without becoming severely depressed or physically ill?

When Jessica stopped to think about what she'd like to achieve while doing this step, she said, "I want my life to be more fulfilling, vibrant, reflective of me, and filled with people who cherish, value, and respect me. This means I need to start saying no to perceived obligations, inertia, lethargy, fear, and mistreatment by others."

But before Jessica could know which boundaries she needed, she had to look at what she wants more of in her life. That's the next step for you too! When you envision a life that contains much more of what you love and want— while containing much *less* of what you *don't* want—you'll inevitably begin to gather the courage to set boundaries.

It happens almost automatically once we can imagine a better version of life for ourselves. Suddenly, the places where we've exchanged our happiness for someone else's stand out in relief. What previously whispered to us begins to roar. Then, the moment arrives when we can no longer tolerate being the doormat for a single moment more. In the meantime, you can prepare for this moment by consciously and proactively imagining what you want more of in your life. That's what this next exercise is all about.

EXERCISE

Your Desire List

In this exercise, you will explore what you desire in your life. What do you want more of? What do you want less of? Then, you'll evaluate whether an unset boundary is what is in the way of having what you want. Write down your answers to the questions in a journal or on a device of your choice.

1. Make a list of what you would like to *increase* or *introduce* in your life. List 5 to 10 desires, including both material and nonmaterial things. They can be large or small, but they must be specific. If you want more money, specify an amount. If you want to travel more, name where you want

to go and how many trips you want to take per year. If you want certain relationships to be more supportive of you, write down how you want to feel in those relationships. If you want more time to yourself, specify when and the activities you'd like to do.

2. Make a list of anything you would like to *decrease* or *release* from your life. Again, list 5 to 10 material and nonmaterial desires, and be specific. If you'd like to spend less time with your in-laws, write down your vision for that (e.g., I don't want to go on vacation with them but would be fine seeing them during the holidays). If you want to work less overtime at work, how much overtime is your upper limit? If you want less conflict with your children, specify the nature of the conflicts you want to resolve and how you want those relationships to feel afterward.

3. Look at each item on both lists, and ask yourself this question: *What boundary could I set in order to get more of what I want and/or less of what I don't want?* Next to the item, write down the boundary that needs to be set in order for you to make this change.

4. Add any new boundaries you discovered from this exercise to your Boundary Pyramid. Put them in their appropriate spots—cherry-on-top, good-to-have, or bottom-line boundaries.

Contemplate the Alternative

Over and over, I watch my clients focus on the consequences they're afraid will result if they set boundaries, rather than the opportunities that would open up if they did. We all fear change and uncertainty. It's only human to anticipate danger, in hopes we can avoid it entirely. That's why it's such a change of pace to focus on the positive consequences of setting boundaries, as we just did in the last exercise. And it's equally important to keep the option on the table of not making any changes at all.

But before you make the decision between staying the course and making change, I want you to be fully informed. That's why the next step in this process is to imagine what life would be like if you *never* set your bottom-line boundaries. What would life look like 3, 5, or 10 years from now—if you decided not to rock the boat at all?

In case you're indulging in the fantasy that the situation will change spontaneously and for the better, let me give you a reality check. It can be tempting to simply suspend our disbelief, hoping the situation will right itself without any action on our part—or with the same action we've been trying, unsuccessfully, for years. We pray she will change or that he will wake up and realize what a jerk he's been. I'm sure I don't need to be the one to break it to you by now, but this kind of miraculous change happens rarely—if ever. Much more likely is that inaction means the situation remains the same as it is now, with no improvement. Whatever frustrates and hurts you now continues to frustrate and hurt you in perpetuity. Sadly, in many cases, the dissatisfaction actually escalates—going from frustrating to enraging to explosive. How many years can you endure your boss's criticism before you can't take it anymore? How long can you remain codependent with your friends, always putting their needs first, before you snap at someone and/or become depressed or ill?

My friend Maddie had to set a difficult boundary with her controlling mother and mentally ill father when she moved from the South to New York City as a young woman. Knowing her parents, she was prepared for drama when she broke the news of her move to them. So she got her plane ticket and found a place to live before she even told them of her plans.

As she suspected, they were very upset and tried to change her mind. But Maddie knew she had to leave. At the time, she believed her move was about pursuing a career as an actress. Many years later, however, she realizes it was for her very survival. If she had stayed, she would have struggled to live her own life on her own terms. She honestly questions if she would still be alive if she had continued to live close to her parents. Getting out of their control and away from their emotional toxicity was the smartest move she ever made, and it required setting a very courageous boundary that said, "This is my life, and I get to decide where I live."

Now it's your turn. What would your future look like if you chose to set *none* of the boundaries on your pyramid? What desired outcomes did you write down in the last exercise that would never come to fruition? What would you to continue to experience in your life that you *don't* want?

Imagining a potential future without much-needed boundaries in place is far from a pleasant thought, but therein lies the power of this exercise. If you don't think about what's truly at stake for you, it's too easy to take the less confrontational road, falling back into your old patterns and telling yourself that you can get by without setting the boundaries that frighten you. Creating this "Ghost of Christmas Future" vision will also make it easier for you to envision your best possible future at the end of this chapter. So with bravery and a deep breath, let's take an honest look at what it would look like to maintain the status quo.

EXERCISE
The No-Boundary Alternative

In this exercise, I'll ask you first to close your eyes in a meditation and imagine your life without any of the boundaries you're thinking of setting. Then, you'll write down what you've envisioned, so you can refer to it whenever your fears try to tell you that you'll be better off without your boundaries. Along with the positive future that you'll envision at the end of the chapter, this exercise will serve as a cautionary tale to buoy your courage and strengthen your resolve to set the boundaries you need for yourself.

For the meditation portion, be sure to turn off all phones so that you can surrender to the process. Wear unrestricting clothes, and sit in a comfortable chair or couch. Feel free to play soft music or light candles, if you like. It helps to record your own voice reading the steps so that you don't have to open your eyes, which will disrupt your meditative state. (You may wish to skip the italicized portions of the meditation when recording.)

For the exercise in Part 2, you will need your journal or preferred device.

Part 1: Meditation on a Future without Boundaries

1. Close your eyes, and take several deep breaths. Relax each part of your body, starting with your feet. Then gradually move up your legs, hips, belly, chest, back, arms, neck, and head until you feel fully relaxed. *Don't work too hard at this. Just ask your body to relax. As you continue, it will relax more and more.*

2. When you're ready, with your eyes closed, picture or feel yourself in the home where you're currently living. It's five years into the future. Allow yourself to smell the scents, hear the sounds, and feel the air. You're in the middle of dealing with one of your most profound boundary issues— perhaps one that has been going on for years. *Maybe someone is putting you down, or you're just expected to take care of something that has become your responsibility for no good reason.* Imagine that you have *not* set a boundary around this issue, so there's been no improvement—or worse, that it has escalated in some way. Allow your imagination to take over and create a potential scene.

3. Now, fast-forward another five years into the future, 10 years from today. Notice what it would be like to have lived with this infringement on your boundary for a full decade beyond today. What does life look and feel like? What do you notice about your own emotional state? Your physical health? How has this affected your life during the last 10 years? Give yourself plenty of time to imagine it vividly.

4. Choose a second major boundary from your pyramid. Picture yourself with the person or people involved in this second situation. This boundary has also never been set, and it is now 10 years beyond the present. How does it feel to have lived with this second issue for an additional decade without any resolution? What do you feel both emotionally and physically, and how has this situation affected your life during the last decade? *I know this can be an uncomfortable, and perhaps even painful, vision to contemplate. So you don't have to stay here for long. Just stay long enough to get a sense of what life would be like, long-term, with the boundaries that are currently causing you pain.*

5. When you feel you have stayed in the vision long enough, wiggle your toes and roll your head to begin to come back to full waking consciousness. Take a deep breath, and open your eyes when you're ready.

Part 2: Write Your Vision of a Life without Boundaries

1. Now that you've had a taste of what life would be like if you never set the most important boundaries in your life, take some notes to help you remember what you experienced in the meditation.

2. Take special care to write down how you felt emotionally, and if you noticed any physical repercussions as a result of not setting these boundaries.

3. Keep these notes. Whenever you want to set a difficult boundary but start to talk yourself out of it, refer back to what you've written in this exercise. It will help you make a decision about the boundary that isn't based in fear of the consequences with the other person. You'll remind yourself that there are also consequences to yourself as a result of *not* setting boundaries.

Remember that it's always your choice whether or not to set a boundary. But it is also you who must live with the consequences of that choice. Don't sell yourself short.

An Empowered Vision of Your Future

You've now seen what your future might look like if you fail to set the boundaries you want to set. Pretty grim, right? Oddly enough, looking at how setting our boundaries would *improve* our future can be no less difficult. Our codependent patterns—overgiving, prioritizing others over ourselves, avoiding conflict at all costs—were installed and maintained for good reasons. It can make for a dissonant and painful experience to imagine our lives without these safety mechanisms in place, even if the new vision finds us happier and more fulfilled. So don't be surprised if you find yourself having *even more resistance* to envisioning a satisfying, joyous future than you did imagining the status quo in the last exercise. This is completely normal and expected.

That said, only when we've fully imagined our desired future can we take the appropriate action steps to claim it as our own and see clearly that short-term discomfort is a small price to pay for the long-term change we crave.

When my client Sharon imagines a future where her boundaries are firmly in place, she immediately senses how free and happy she will be. "I will stop obsessing about the reactions of others. I will spend my time thinking, *What do I want today?* and then taking actions to make that happen. I will focus on *me* and what I need to do in order to create the freedom and happiness I want so much."

Elaine envisions an effortless flow of "energy, time, joy, ease, and freedom" in her life. "In the areas I struggle with, the angst will melt away," she says. "My creativity will explode because I won't worry about the judgments from others or myself. My words and actions will be in perfect alignment. I will put myself first, and not think doing so is selfish. I will so love and adore myself that I will glisten! From a practical perspective, my day-to-day life will have boundaries. I will be rock solid on what I charge clients, knowing how much the work I do will impact their lives."

Candace puts her vision of boundary badassery simply: "I will allow my life and the way I live it to stand alone—on its own merit."

In Valerie's vision, she says, "I will be at peace with myself. I will have compassion for others whose lives are affected by my boundary setting, but I will know it's the right thing for me to do. I imagine speaking my truth with calmness, sincerity, and conviction because I'll be in alignment with myself. Thinking, speaking, and acting will be one and the same. I will feel my own power and the strength that comes from a self-directed life, however many 'mistakes' and corrections I might have to make along the way. It will be *my* life."

There are infinite positive possibilities that await each of us when we dare to claim our needs and prioritize our desires. We might even end up creating an entirely new life for ourselves—like me or my friend, who left her controlling childhood home and built a life she loves in New York.

Similarly, my client Zoe left her first marriage in 1998, and it was an enormous act of courage for her. "I remember walking out the door and my ex saying to me, 'You'll never go through with this; what are you going to do without me?' Today, that statement makes me laugh out loud. But at the time, I thought, 'I don't know . . . but I do know I can't stay any longer.' It was the first time I ever chose me. It took a while to peel myself away from my patterns, but it was the best decision I ever made." Today, she's married to a kind and loving man, with whom she has a beautiful daughter. At the time she left her first marriage, she couldn't see the possibility of this new life she's created, but it's infinitely better than anything she had in the past.

Again, setting a boundary doesn't necessarily require that we take such drastic action as Zoe or I did. But it does require that we have some faith in what's possible for us. It requires that we believe in a potential outcome that we may not yet have the capacity to comprehend.

In the meditation and exercise that follow, I ask you to imagine what your life will be like when you've finished setting all the boundaries in your pyramid. When each and every one is honored and respected, without conflict. For the purposes of this meditation, I'm going to ask you for a leap of faith: I want you to imagine that everyone you know and love is perfectly okay with your boundaries as stated, and that you feel no guilt or shame about setting any of them. This may sound far-fetched, but it isn't as improbable as you think. Our fear can distort our future vision to the point where we can't imagine our requests going over well. In truth, your family, friends, and co-workers are likely to be far less upset than you think.

At the heart of the matter, acknowledging, setting, and maintaining boundaries is about taking concrete steps to create the life you most want. You are the one with the power here, which is why I'm calling this your "empowered vision."

EXERCISE
Create Your Empowered Vision

This exercise has four parts. The first part is a meditation, followed by three writing exercises.

For the meditation portion, be sure to turn off all phones so that you can surrender to the process. Wear unrestricting clothes, and sit in a comfortable chair or couch. Feel free to play soft music or light candles, if you like. It helps to record your own voice reading the steps so that you don't have to open your eyes, which will disrupt your meditative state. (You may wish to skip the italicized portions of the meditation in your recording.)

For the writing portions, have your journal or device handy.

Part 1: Meditation on the Future

1. Close your eyes, and take several deep breaths. Relax each part of your body, starting with your feet. Then gradually move up your legs, hips, belly, chest, back, arms, neck, and head until you feel fully relaxed. *Don't work too hard at this. Just ask your body to relax. As you continue, it will relax more and more.*

2. When you're ready, with your eyes closed, picture or feel yourself in your home five years in the future. You might be living in your current home or a new place. Allow yourself to smell the scents, hear the sounds, and feel the air. The key people in your personal life are there with you, and you have set every boundary in your pyramid. There has been no conflict, guilt, or shame related to your boundary setting, and you now set boundaries easily and effortlessly in the moment as they come up. What do you feel emotionally? Physically? How has this change in you affected your home life?

3. Imagine yourself at work now. You may be in your current job or a different one. How has your professional life been affected by setting your most important boundaries? What is different in your life? How do you feel emotionally, physically, mentally, and spiritually?

4. Envision yourself with your extended family. Perhaps you're spending the holidays together. How is this time with them different from the past, now that you've set all of the boundaries you've wanted to set?

5. Finally, imagine yourself in a social situation with friends. What's different about this aspect of your life now that you're a skilled and confident boundary setter?

6. Stay in this vision as long as you like. When you're ready, wiggle your toes and roll your head to begin to come back to full waking consciousness. Then, open your eyes.

Part 2: Write Your Vision of Your Life as a Boundary Badass

1. Now that you've had a taste of what life would be like with all of your boundaries in place, write this vision down. Make note of everything you can remember from the meditation so that you won't forget it. Don't expect to rely on your memory alone—write down the details!

2. Take special care to note how you felt emotionally. Did you feel empowered? At peace? Content? Free?

Part 3: Your List of Exhilarating Outcomes (LEO)

1. From what you discovered in the meditation, make a list of all of the positive changes you foresee in your life when your boundaries have been set. This is your List of Exhilarating Outcomes (LEO). For example, you might write:

- *I feel free and have less stress because I no longer take responsibility for the feelings of others.*

- *I don't spend time with my in-laws, which allows me to finally enjoy my holidays and make beautiful memories with my kids.*

2. Keep your LEO and other notes some-where safe. In the future, whenever you need to set a difficult boundary, refer back to what you've written in this exercise. Just like the no-boundary vision, rereading your best-case scenario will help you make a decision about the boundary that isn't based in fear of the consequences with the other person.

Part 4: Pledge to Yourself

1. In this final portion of the exercise, write a pledge to yourself as follows: "I consciously choose to have the life I'm envisioning. I see that to have it, I must become a boundary badass. I deserve the life I most desire, and do not need to feel guilty about it. I will be brave and follow through at my own pace until I have set all the boundaries I need in order to give myself the love and respect I deserve." Then, sign your pledge and keep it in a safe place where you will see it often.

Can you feel your confidence and courage growing? I swear I can feel it, all the way over here! That means just one thing: it's time to start thinking of the *how*. What will you actually *say* when you set your boundaries? That's what Step 7 is all about: setting some guidelines for how, specifically, you will put your boundaries into words.

REMEMBER

When you contemplate whether
or not to set a boundary, recall your
vision of a life as a champion boundary
setter, as well as your life without
this boundary in place.

WRITE YOUR SCRIPTS

Laura's husband had a habit of getting up early in the mornings so that the two of them could connect, but the morning hours didn't really lend themselves to meaningful connection time. He was tired, and she was preoccupied. Instead, their morning ritual only caused Laura to feel anxious and stressed. She realized what she really needed was three mornings a week to spend some time by herself.

She set the following boundary with her husband: "I've noticed that when you get up in the morning to spend time with me, it actually brings up anxiety instead of connection. In order to make myself more comfortable, I'm going to spend Monday, Wednesday, and Friday mornings alone, distraction-free. If I become distracted, I'll leave the house early." Obviously, she said this lovingly and without anger or blame, but as you can see, she kept it short, sweet, and direct.

My client Kim and her ex-husband have been butting heads over the care of their children. He lets them get away with eating unhealthy foods and not finishing their homework, which has caused their grades to suffer. He also lets them go to parties without consulting Kim first. In order to try to rectify the situation, Kim set a boundary with him: "I'm grateful for your financial support as stated in our parenting plan and for what your family contributes, but I'd like for us to work together to raise our children with consistency. This will require that we talk and collaborate regularly. I suggest we meet every six to eight weeks to discuss our kids' needs and our respective financial responsibilities. Are you willing and available to do this?"

Stephanie's boyfriend had a habit of smoking cannabis in her home, so she set a boundary in this way: "When you smoke cannabis at my place, I feel resentful because I don't like the smell and how it lingers in the house even when you smoke outside. Would you be willing to use your cannabis vape pen instead since the smell is less pronounced?" Note that she focused on how *she* feels about his smoking. She didn't point an accusatory finger at him. Should he have protested, she could negotiate a different option to get the same outcome, asking him to take a walk around the block when he smokes, rather than doing it right outside the front door.

Jessica's husband convinced her to get a dog, saying that he wanted a dog to take on walks and runs. But before long, her husband stopped walking the dog, and Jessica took on the responsibility since she didn't want the dog to be neglected. This quickly caused her to feel resentful, so she decided to set a boundary: "I'm feeling frustrated when you don't walk the dog like you said you would when we bought her," Jessica told her husband. "It isn't a responsibility I wanted, so I'd appreciate it if you would take her out like you promised."

His response was simply, "Oh, okay." But if he had said he wouldn't do it, Jessica could have said, "If you won't take responsibility for the dog as you promised, we will have to find her another home because I'm not willing to walk her anymore." That would be a hard line to take, but the alternative would be to build up resentment toward her husband that could poison their relationship in irreparable ways.

Sharon hired an assistant who sent her multiple e-mails every day asking questions. First, Sharon recognized that she needed to give the assistant clearer direction, so she set a weekly meeting to address less pressing questions. In order to set the boundary regarding the e-mails, she said, "If you send an e-mail with a question, I will respond when I'm available within 24 hours. If the question isn't urgent, however, please compile a list of questions for us to discuss in our weekly meeting." Setting this boundary has spared Sharon from the e-mail interruptions during her day.

These are examples of some of the scripts my clients used to set their boundaries. Many people I know have avoided setting boundaries simply because they weren't sure what to say. So in this step—*Write Your Scripts*—you will decide on the words you'll use to set one or more of your boundaries. By choosing your words in advance, you'll be prepared to set the boundary with no guesswork and hopefully no hesitation. You'll also be less likely to become derailed by your emotions in the moment.

Boundary Language Guidelines

Gabrielle used to try to set boundaries with her husband to no avail. "The circular disagreements with him would leave me in tears," she says. "I could not make a simple point. He would counterattack and then come back and ask me to defend myself. When I'd respond, he'd counterattack again. It was a no-win situation, until I was in tears and apologizing." Sometimes, he wouldn't let it go and would put her down, telling her she was wrong, stupid, and cruel, even after she apologized.

One of the reasons many of my clients have shied away from setting boundaries is the fear of having an experience like Gabrielle's. They've tried to make their wishes known, only to end up in arguments with their loved ones. Most of the time, this can be avoided by following some basic language guidelines. There are times, of course, when trying to set a boundary with someone is never going to work. This is especially true with people who are narcissists or suffering from borderline personality disorder. In these cases, they simply aren't capable of honoring boundaries or having a rational discussion about them. If you're in a relationship with someone who has mental health issues, it's especially important not to engage in a discussion about your boundaries with them. It will be up to you to maintain your boundaries as best you can with people like this, and in some instances, that might mean extracting yourself from the relationship entirely.

If you're engaging with a rational person, however, about your boundary issue, it's also important to avoid overexplaining your position. "I have a tendency to explain everything," Elaine says. "I can't tell you how many times I've erased a text or e-mail because I've offered far too much information about my decision than the other person needed to hear."

Renee even had an interviewer tell her she was too transparent, which caused her to think about the boundaries of what, when, where, and how to share information. Often, when we overshare or overexplain, we're hoping to buffer potential conflict, or we're looking for approval and validation from the other person.

In his communication methodology known as Nonviolent Communication (NVC), Marshall Rosenberg says that we are the gatekeepers of how much information we share. It's our choice to share as much or as little as we want. When it comes to boundary setting, less is more.

You aren't obligated to explain yourself. Say what you need to say—and then stop!

If you remember nothing more from this chapter, please remember these two directives:

> ***Express no more—and no less—***
> ***than the boundary you want and need.***
> ***"No" is a complete sentence.***

If someone makes a request of you and you reply, "No," that person may very well wait, expecting you to explain why. Just because someone wants an explanation from you, there's no obligation to offer it. "I think people are so trained to hear an excuse after the 'no' that it stops them in their tracks," Zoe says. But that isn't a reason for you to say anything more unless you feel moved to do so.

If you feel that you *must* say something more than that one word—such as in answer to your boss, for example—keep it simple, such as, "No, I'm not available for that," or "No, that doesn't work for me." Often, on a subconscious level, people will respect you even more because they can tell you're speaking from your truth.

Often, we continue far beyond the word *no* because we feel a need to be understood, which is actually a need for approval. So avoid making being understood so important that it dilutes the power of your choice. If you choose to say more than "no," don't do it because you're afraid of conflict or disapproval.

For example, let's say you've been spending time with someone whose company you don't enjoy. You haven't wanted to be hurtful, but you really don't want to hang out anymore. The next time the person asks you to do something together, you might want to say more than *no* in an effort to be kind. But you still don't need to offer a lengthy explanation. You could simply say, "I've appreciated our time together, but my life is very full and busy. So I'm not able to make any new plans for the foreseeable future."

I have a simple format for setting my own boundaries when others are involved. It consists of two parts: a request, and if necessary, a declaration of intention. The request includes a statement of the other person's impact—"I feel X, when you do or say Y"—followed by a direct request. I think of it as Plan A. The hope is that the other person will hear you, understand, and be willing and able to keep the boundary you're requesting. Here are a few examples of requests, stated in my preferred format:

- I feel frustrated and taken for granted, when you don't wash your dishes. Are you willing to do your own dishes going forward?

- I feel angry and uncomfortable when your brother makes racist comments. I don't want to see him socially except at family gatherings. Does that work for you?

- I feel resentful because I end up having to clean up after your dog, when he crosses the street and poops in my yard. Will you please figure out a way to keep your dog in your own yard?

In the best-case scenario, the other person will say, "I'm so sorry! I didn't realize how my actions were affecting you. I will absolutely do better going forward." Alas, we don't always get the ideal response. So if the other party is unable or unwilling to meet your request, the next step is to move on to Plan B: you take care of you. This is when you let the other party know how you're going to handle the situation moving forward in order to get your needs met. Remember, it's never anyone else's responsibility to keep your boundary; that job is yours and yours alone. For every situation, you'll need to have a backup plan in place *before* you make your boundary request—a plan for how you, yourself, will make sure your boundary is honored. Here are some Plan B examples, based on the boundary requests mentioned:

- Since you won't wash your own dishes, I'm going to use some of the household budget to purchase paper plates so I don't have to wash them for you.

- Since you still want to see your brother socially, I will simply stay home.

- Since you are not willing to keep your dog in your own yard, I will plan to call animal control when I next see him coming into my yard.

In most cases, it's a good idea to make your request first to determine if the other person is in agreement before you state what you'll do if the behavior or expectation happens again. Use your discernment, however, to determine if a request will work. If it's a contentious relationship, direct requests might be difficult and could open a door to a bigger argument. You may have tried repeatedly before and failed; if so, skip it. Moreover, abusive or narcissistic people won't be capable of meeting you in a collaborative way. In that case, you will probably need to simply state the action you are taking to keep your boundary—and not make a request at all.

Here are some additional guidelines for your boundary language scripting:

- **Avoid language that blames the other person.** Remember that *you* are the one who has been infringing on your own boundaries by letting this go on so long. It's your job to see to it that your limits are honored going forward. If you're upset, you may have to work hard to keep your anger in check, but it's worth it. If you say something accusatory, you'll open the door for an argument that will do more harm than good. So own the situation. You've been crossing your own boundary by allowing circumstances that are doing you harm, and you are now strong in your resolve to set the new boundary.

- **Try to keep the focus on yourself and your feelings.** Using *I* statements, reveal how you feel about the situation and what you'd like to do to rectify it. While you may need to briefly mention the other person's behavior, bring it right back to yourself and how you feel as a result.

- **Avoid self-blame, and only apologize if you truly feel you need to do so.** There are times when an apology is merited, but too often, we apologize because we're uncomfortable. There is no need to apologize when we've done nothing to harm the other person. Remember: You aren't at fault if you're taking care of your own needs. You aren't doing harm in refusing to attend to another's unreasonable demands. If your tendency is to take on more responsibility than you deserve, watch this habit closely. I know it can be difficult to say no without also saying sorry, but I have made it my practice to stop myself when I'm tempted to say it. Avoid getting caught up in showing more empathy to others than you show for your own needs.

Doing so sends a mixed message that weakens and dilutes your position, as well as your resolve that you deserve to set your boundary.

- **Avoid self-righteous language.** Pointing fingers never gets us anywhere good. For example, you're likely to cause an argument if you say something like, "I'm the one who has been picking up your dirty laundry for God knows how long," or "I'm not the one who drinks too much when we go to parties." Stick to the script and to your own feelings.

- **Don't make excuses for yourself.** There is no need to justify *why* you need a boundary. For example, you don't have to say, "I can't afford to loan you money anymore." You simply need to state that you aren't going to provide loans going forward. If the person asks why, simply respond that you're no longer willing to do so. You're under no obligation to provide a reason or justification.

- **Don't make empty threats.** Crying wolf only serves to weaken your resolve—and your self-trust. If you say you're going to leave the party if your husband has more than two drinks, you need to leave the next time it happens. If you ask for a raise, don't threaten to quit if you don't get it. That is, unless you're prepared to do so!

Anchor the Positive Outcomes

In an Oprah.com story, Brené Brown said that whenever she's preparing to set a boundary, she creates an anchor. Her choice is to turn a ring on her finger while repeating to herself, *Choose discomfort over resentment,* as a reminder that she's going through short-term discomfort in exchange for long-term relief.

When you get ready to set your boundary with another person, I recommend choosing some physical action like this that you can do in any situation without being noticed. It will remind you *why* you're setting your boundary and help you to feel empowered to see it through. Here are some possibilities:

- Turn your ring, watch, or bracelet.

- Tap your leg with a finger or two.

- Gently press your nails into your palm to remind yourself to stay present and in your body.

- Carry a stone or crystal in your pocket, and pull it out to hold in your palm.

It might even be helpful to use your anchor as you practice what you're going to say. Use this action with your anchor to fill you with courage. As you turn your ring or whatever you do during your script practice, you will create a memory of courage that you can then take into the actual moment you set your boundary.

What anchor will you set?

Phrases for Setting Boundaries

After working on her boundaries, Sharon went on a blind date with a man she met on an online dating app. When they met in person, she saw immediately that he was at least 20 years older than her—and realized that he'd lied on his profile. She wasn't sure at first how she felt about it, so when he asked if she'd like to go out again, she said, "I'm committed to being honest, and I'm having a hard time with the age difference. Give me 24 hours to think about it." Within 24 hours, Sharon realized that it was a definite no. In the past, she would have immediately agreed to another date in order to avoid hurting the man's feelings.

As my client Tina puts it, "I don't say yes right away to anything anymore, unless it's a full-body, absolute yes." Remember, an inauthentic yes to someone else is a no to yourself and what *you* want.

I find that a good way to practice checking in with your authentic feelings is to tell yourself you're *not allowed to say yes to anything* without a waiting period. Even if you know you want to accept an invitation, challenge yourself to pause. Here are some phrases you can use for this assignment:

"Thanks for asking. I'll check my schedule and get back to you."

"I appreciate the invitation. I'll sleep on it and let you know."

"It sounds like fun. Let me check on a few things and text you tomorrow."

Consider memorizing these phrases, so you'll always have them in your back pocket. Then, think of it as a game—patting yourself on the back anytime you remember to use one of these.

Here are some more phrases for different situations to help you get started setting your boundaries when a short and sweet reply makes sense:

To Say No:

"Thanks for asking, but I'm not available for that."

"I appreciate the invitation, but I won't be able to make it."

"I love the offer, but I'll have to take a rain check."

To Halt Unsolicited Feedback or Criticism:

"I'm not open to your comments about my weight."

"I'm not seeking input about my appearance."

"I'm not interested in opinions about my life decisions."

To Make a Direct Request:

"Tonight, I'd like to choose where we have dinner."

"I'd like to spend one night each week in the guest bedroom alone, as I sleep better on my own."

"I'd like to enlist the help of an assistant to complete the new project."

To Pause for Reflection:

"I'm upset right now and want to revisit this once we're both calm."

"This conversation seems to be doing more harm than good. I'm going to go to the other room for 15 minutes and then come back and check in with you." (Then make sure you keep your word and come back in 15!)

"I will take 24 hours to sleep on this and get back to you with what I want to do."

Your "Company Line"

Priya recently went through a breakup, and her family has been insisting she share the details of what happened. Why would you just end the relationship? Have you spoken to him? Aren't you trying to work it out? What did he do that's so terrible? Why wouldn't you want to avoid a divorce? Since it's customary in her family for everyone to know each other's business, it has been hard for her to set the boundary that feels right—i.e., stay private about the details. So she's found herself trying to explain without revealing everything, or just answering their questions with, "I don't know."

But Priya doesn't owe her family an explanation just because they think she does.

She needs what I call a "company line"—a sentence or two that clearly sets her boundary, which she can repeat as many times as necessary. In this case, for example, Priya's company line might be: "The decision to break up feels right to me, and I'm not interested in sharing more details about it." No matter how many times a family member tries to open up the conversation, she can go back to her company line. Eventually, people will get tired of hearing the same answer.

Sure, her family might get upset with her for not spilling the beans, but *c'est la vie*. They don't have a right to interfere in her personal affairs. If she caves in and tells them what they want to hear, she will feel resentful. She'll also open herself to more criticism—the familiar dynamic in her family. Priya's pattern is to ask for a boundary and then later give in, seeking approval. But as all of us know, the only person whose approval should matter to Priya is Priya's. She doesn't have to justify her life choices to anyone else, and just because someone asks doesn't mean she has to answer. But after so many years of relenting, it can be challenging to change without a lot of support. This is where the company line especially comes in handy.

Your company line is a great way to avoid getting into a debate about the boundary. You simply say it and then stop talking. And it's an easy way to continue to uphold your boundary whenever it's crossed again—you just reiterate it as often as necessary. In the first conversation, you might have to repeat it several times before it hits home with the other person. This is especially true if you're switching gears after a long stretch of time where you didn't assert this boundary or even mention you had one at all.

Often, your company line can be your Plan B line from the beginning of this chapter. "If you do X, I will take care of myself by doing Y."

We usually set boundaries with people we know pretty well, so we can pretty easily imagine what they're going to say in response. As you prepare your script and get ready for the big conversation, think of a few different possible responses you might get back. Aaron Rodgers of the Green Bay Packers football team has said that he isn't nervous when he takes to the field because he has already run all of the potential plays in his head and is prepared for almost every possible scenario. Take a page from his playbook as you get ready to set your boundary. I recommend making a list of possible ways the conversation might go: "If they

say or do _____, then I will say or do _____."
(What you say most of the time in response will be your company line!)

Of course, we never know exactly how it's going to go; I find that many of my clients are pleasantly surprised by the response they get. But regardless, the more prepared you are, the more confident you'll feel when you sit down. And confidence is the key to following through.

So think of me as your coach, running plays with you in the locker room before the big game. Let's go over some possible scripts—and the conversations that might result. For this example, let's imagine you've got a brother who has a habit of coming over for unannounced visits, and you're ready to set a boundary.

You: "It's inconvenient when you come over without calling first because it interrupts tasks I need to get done. Are you willing to call first so that I can let you know if it's a good time for you to visit?"

Brother: "But I thought you liked spending time with me."

You: "I do enjoy spending time with you, but I have things I have to do without interruption. In the future, I'll need you to call before you come over. If you come over unannounced, in order to take care of myself and finish my work, I won't be able to answer the door."

Brother: "Well, that would be rude of you."

You: [Here's the company line:] "I'm happy to visit with you if you call first to plan ahead."

Brother: "So much for spontaneity!"

You: "I'm happy to visit with you if you call first to plan ahead."

Brother: "But we've never done it like that."

You: "This is what I need now to take care of myself. I'm happy to visit with you if you call first to plan ahead."

Brother: "Okay, okay—you're happy to visit with me if I call first to plan ahead!"

You: "Exactly! Thank you."

Note how "you" avoided getting into a deep discussion with your brother or arguing with his attempts at manipulation and guilt. "You" simply repeated the company line of "I'm happy to visit with you if you call first to plan ahead."

While the brother in this scenario might be prickly about the arrangement for a while, chances are he would get over it eventually. If not, the "you" would have to be prepared for Plan B: To not to answer the door when he shows up unexpectedly.

Here's another potential conversation between two best friends, where the friend with the boundary makes her request before stating her company line:

Friend #1: "When you ask to borrow money, I feel uncomfortable. As much as I love you, I need you to stop asking me for money."

Friend #2: "But I've always counted on you to help me out."

Friend #1: "I know, but I'm not comfortable helping financially anymore."

Friend #2: "But why? I know you have the money."

Friend #1: "It's what I need now, and I need you to respect my decision." (Notice how she does not go into apologies, conversations about her own financial situation, or any explanation or excuse. She simply names her need.)

Friend #2: "Well, I don't know what I'm going to do without your help. Don't you care what happens to me?"

Friend #1: "Of course I do. [Here's the company line:] But if you ask me for money in the future, I will end the conversation."

Friend #2: "If you needed money and I had it, I would give it to you in a heartbeat."

Friend #1: "If you ask me for money in the future, I will end the conversation." (Notice how she does not engage the guilt trip her friend is trying to lay on her. She goes straight to her company line.)

Friend #1 is taking a hard line, yes, and this type of scenario might indeed end the friendship. This is the kind of scenario that my clients dread. But once they've taken it, they feel *so much better*. What kind of friendship do you have with someone who expects things you don't want to give?

So what do you do if the conversation becomes heated? My friend Elizabeth ran into just this situation. She had endured years of disdain and anger from her sister about a misstep she'd made a decade earlier. Elizabeth had apologized, genuinely, on three separate occasions—but her sister would not let it go, and the abuse continued almost every time they were together. Elizabeth knew she had to set a hard boundary, saying, "You will not treat me like this even one more time, or you won't see me again." But she loved her sister and was terrified of losing her.

The final straw came in the form of an e-mail, in which her sister laid into her for her decision not to come home for the holidays. Elizabeth picked up the phone and called her sister. She kicked the hornet's nest right away by saying, "You seemed upset with me about my travel decision." Her sister, per usual, started berating her immediately. Here's how the conversation went from there:

Elizabeth: *(Interrupting)* I'm going to pause you right here. This thing that's happening right now, where you're yelling at me, this is never going to happen again. I do not allow myself to be treated this way by anyone in my life except you. But I've hit my limit. You will treat me with kindness and respect going forward, or you will not see me again.

Sister: *(Angry)* I don't know what you're talking about! You are the most selfish person—

Elizabeth: *(Interrupting again)* I'm talking about what's happening right this minute, where you are yelling at me and telling me I'm selfish and irresponsible and only think about myself. That's not true, and you're the only person in my life who would ever say that to me. You think you can treat me this way because I'm your sister, but going forward you will treat me like you treat your friends. Do not think of me as your sister anymore. If you can't treat me with the same respect you bring to your friends, you will not have me in your life anymore.

Sister: *(Long pause, then crying)* You are right. You're right. I don't know why I treat you this way. I love you. I just get so angry at you.

Elizabeth: *(Crying)* I love you so much, and I don't want to lose you. If you're upset with me, I'm open to a rational conversation about just about anything. But I'm no longer open to getting yelled at and told what a bad person I am.

Sister: You are totally right. I understand. I'm going to work on it.

Elizabeth was truly blown away by how easy the conversation went once she was brave enough to have it. She'd let herself sit in the line of fire for years, worried about launching into an even bigger conflict. But the minute she asserted her boundary—and was prepared to stick to her company line of cutting her sister out of her life—her sister backed down, apologized, and changed her ways. To this day, they have never had a problem again.

Here's another scenario in which a man struggles to set a boundary with his wife. While I suggested you avoid overexplaining, you may want to explain yourself a *little* bit when the conversation is happening with someone who's very important to you. Again, just be careful not to explain from a place of defensiveness, apology, excuses, or the need for approval. Whatever you do, don't fall into the trap of defending your boundary in order to make sure the other person feels okay. That isn't your responsibility. Explain from an empowered place, reminding yourself that you're entitled to your boundaries, and go back to your company line as quickly as you can. *Clarify, but don't defend.*

This is also where your anchor will come in handy!

Husband: "In the past, I've asked for time to myself, but I haven't maintained that boundary. From now on, in order to take care of myself, I'm going to spend Saturday mornings by myself."

Wife: "I don't understand why you want to get away from me."

Husband: "I don't want to get away from you; I just need a little time alone."

Wife: "It makes me feel like you don't love me."

Husband: "You know I love you, but it's also healthy to have some time to ourselves. I will spend four hours by myself each Saturday morning. If it doesn't work for me to stay at the house for my alone time, I'll go somewhere else."

Wife: "If you go somewhere else, how do I know you aren't meeting another woman?"

Husband: "I'll go somewhere else to have time *alone.*"

Wife: "Why are you doing this?"

Husband: "It's what I need."

Wife: "What about what *I* need?"

Husband: "Your needs are your own responsibility. I'm open to hearing them, but I'll ask you to respect my needs equally. I love you, and I enjoy your company. From now on, to take care of myself, I'll spend my Saturday mornings alone."

Now you have an idea of some potential scripts. Of course, create your own scripts that work in your life and for your relationships. These are just examples to help you write your own.

In the next exercise, we'll write a script for one of your bottom-line boundaries, but you don't have to set it yet! In fact, I recommend you don't. This is just the preparation, and there's more to come to set you up for the best possible outcome when you *do* set your boundary.

EXERCISE

Write Your Script

In this exercise, you'll choose one of your bottom-line boundaries from your Boundary Pyramid and write your script in a journal or on a device of your choice.

1. Start with your request (be sure to state what X, Y, and Z stand for). "I feel X, when you do or say Y. Are you willing to not do that?" If the person says no, you will then say, "The next time you do X, I will do Z in order to take care of myself."

2. Even if the other person says yes to your request, you may decide to name your Plan B/company line intention. "If X happens again, I will do Z to take care of myself." This is a good idea if you don't expect the person to live up to their side of the agreement. For example, your father may agree to stop putting your husband down, but it may be a habit that he finds hard to break. It could be that you have already asked him to stop. Therefore, you may want him to know that you're truly serious this time and will take action if he does it again. Then, of course, be prepared to put your company line into action and do what you say you will do. If you say you'll leave the next time he puts down your husband in front of you, then you must be prepared to leave.

3. Write down how you imagine the conversation continuing. What might the other person say in protest, and how do you want to respond? Continue with "If you say or do _____, then I will say or do _____" as many times as necessary to exhaust all possibilities that come to mind. Before you write your responses, however, reread the guidelines earlier in the chapter to make sure you avoid the most common pitfalls, and remember to avoid getting into a drawn-out discussion. Remember that most of the time, your response will be your company line.

4. Find a "Boundary Buddy," if at all possible. This is someone who will be willing to talk with you about the boundaries you're working to set, as you reciprocate for your buddy. This person will

be available to you particularly right before you set a boundary to give you a pep talk, as well as right after to help you decompress emotionally from the experience. I strongly recommend that you take the time to find an appropriate ally for this. As you prepare in the next step to set this important boundary, you will especially need the help of this person.

You've discovered the emotional obstacles standing in your way, and you've explored the consequences of both setting and not setting boundaries. Now that you have script guidelines, you have all the tools you need to begin setting boundaries successfully. Does the idea make you shake in your shoes? Don't worry—we're going to start with your "easier" boundaries first and work our way up to the more challenging ones. You're ready!

REMEMBER

Express no more
—and no less—than the
boundary you want and need.

CHOOSE YOUR "BEGINNER" BOUNDARIES

"I just got a request for a spreadsheet from upper management, and I need you to get me the information by tomorrow," Bob's boss said to him. But when Bob scrolled down and saw the e-mail his boss had received from his own boss, the date was a few days earlier. Clearly, it hadn't "just" been received.

Bob was supposed to have most of the day off on Friday. "I can commit to getting it to you by end of day Thursday, and any edits need to be back to me by 10 A.M. Friday," he told his boss, who agreed to the arrangement.

Around 1 P.M. on Friday, Bob got an e-mail from his boss with the edits. Bob responded, "Based on our agreement, I was to get all changes by 10 A.M. I'm out of the office and unable to make those changes."

What was his boss's response? "You're right. I did make that commitment to you. I will take care of it. Have a great weekend."

In the past, Bob says, he would have dropped everything to get on a computer and make the edits. It wasn't easy for him, but he was proud of himself. "I set a boundary for myself, I stuck to it, and I think I gained respect in the process," he says. Obviously, there are no guarantees that everyone's boss would respond this favorably, but again, I find that our catastrophic expectations rarely pan out.

For Margaret, the boundary she needed to set was with one of her students. "There was a young woman who came to all of my yoga classes and workshops a while back," Margaret says. "She was a total sweetheart. She loved everything I shared, and she just wanted more and more. Then, she started calling me for support. After a few times, I knew I had to set a boundary. So I told her that the best way for me to support her was in class, and if an issue came up, she needed to call a family member or her therapist." While Margaret's student was disappointed, she honored the request and stopped calling.

Margaret recently set another boundary with her parents. "I was getting ready to visit my parents in my home state. I knew they'd have my favorite wine chilling for me in the fridge because they always do. But I'd decided I wasn't drinking for a while. This wasn't easy for me, so the last thing I needed or wanted was a glass of wine handed to me when I arrived in the middle of the afternoon. In the past, I had tried to refrain and then ended up having the wine anyway because I hadn't asked my parents not to offer it to me. This time, I called them ahead of time and told them not to have the wine ready for me like usual. This was the first time I had ever been at my parents' house and not had wine the entire time. Because I was committed and stated my boundary out loud ahead of time, everyone (including me) respected it and was supportive of me. Gaining the awareness, confidence, and skill to speak my truth and set boundaries has been a game changer in all areas of my life."

Megan says she's begun to set boundaries with her son. "When he asks me to take him somewhere or do something for him, I ask myself if it works for me to say yes at that moment. If not, I say I will do it later and propose a time that would work better. It has been a bit of a shock for him, but he goes along with it. This has meant less resentment in my life, and I'm able to complete what I want to do."

Laura is learning to set boundaries that keep her from overgiving. "My mom asked if I'd mind hosting a surprise party for my stepsister. I said I'd be happy to offer the location, but I wouldn't prepare food or drinks. I suggested people bring food potluck style. It worked out! My mom brought the main dish, my dad brought the ice cream, and my brother brought the drinks."

Elaine didn't like that her husband lost his temper at other drivers whenever they were in the car together. Turns out he didn't like it when she used her phone in the car while he was driving. When he told her he feels like a chauffeur when she uses her phone in the car, she used that as an opening to set her boundary against his road rage. Together, they decided that whenever they were in the car, she would drive. This would prevent her from being on the phone, and he wouldn't become angry at other drivers.

These are examples of what I call "beginner boundaries." A beginner boundary is a practice boundary—one you don't think will result in conflict, that doesn't cause you a lot of anxiety, but that you were still scared to set in the past. Usually beginner boundaries live in the cherry-on-top or good-to-have layers on your pyramid, rather than your bottom-line layer. They present an opportunity to stretch a little and use your newly formed boundary-setting muscles without taking a huge risk.

This step is all about choosing, and then setting, one such boundary. Yes, this is the first time I will be asking you to set an actual boundary! But don't worry, I'll be here next to you the whole time. By this point in the book, you've done so much preparation work that I promise it's not going to be as hard as you might think. And it's the first step toward creating a life based on your own design. Let's go!

Practice Makes Awesome

Setting a simple beginner boundary may seem inconsequential, but it's actually a real turning point. I find this step helps clients build confidence and feel more empowered, no matter how small their boundaries may seem. The more comfortable we get setting beginner boundaries, the closer we'll get to setting the most important ones—the boundaries we want and need the most for our health and well-being.

Setting a boundary is a practice in progress. Often, we set a boundary—even a little one—and we have to set it again, and then again! Remember Bob, my client from the beginning of the chapter who had to reset the boundary his boss agreed to about not working on his day off? Same for Jessica, whose son always wants her to drop everything and help him *right now*. The pattern did not stop when she set the boundary the first time; it was her job to maintain it, over and over, even though it was a relatively simple one.

In other words, boundary setting requires small actions repeated many times over long periods. And as one of my clients once said, "Practice makes awesome"—not just in terms of learning to set the boundary in the first place, but also in terms of maintaining it over the course of time. You may begin to feel like a broken record with some people, saying the same thing (like your company line) again and again. But maintenance is an integral part of the boundary-setting process. Understand that "practice makes awesome," and it's easier to let the frustration go.

For your beginner boundaries, your script may be simple. Whatever you choose to say, do it: (1) without apology, (2) without defending your choice, and (3) without casting blame. Keep the focus primarily on yourself, and keep it short and sweet.

For example, say you have a client who always expects you to be available on short notice. A simple boundary might be, "In the future, I will need at least a week's notice to complete work for you."

Say your partner always expects you to do the cooking. You might say, "I've decided I'm only going to cook dinner three nights a week from now on. The other nights, we can go out, or order food in, or you can cook."

What Are "Self-Boundaries"?

For some of my clients, setting a beginner boundary with another person was too much of a challenge. So we inched our way in that direction by first setting what we called "self-boundaries." These are boundaries that you set with yourself instead of with another person.

How many times have you crossed your own boundaries by not living up to commitments you've made to yourself? Maybe you cheated on your diet or procrastinated until you had to work on an assignment at the last minute.

Perhaps you told yourself you wouldn't fill every single night of your week with social engagements, or you promised yourself you'd only have one beer during the game—and then had three. These are examples of the kind of self-boundaries my clients tried on for size before taking on a beginner boundary with someone else.

"I decided I would create a boundary with myself around criticizing my sister for spending money on things I don't agree with," Jessica says. "I made a rule that if we, for example, ever ended up at Target together, I was *not allowed* to comment on what she was buying because it always made me miserable and made her mad." Jessica recognized that her criticism was actually infringing on her sister's boundary, so she created a self-boundary to keep her opinions in check.

Abby and her ex-husband have remained extremely close since their divorce a year ago. "Now that we've both started dating, it's become clear that we need space from each other," she says. "Still, it's been really hard to keep that boundary with him. He's my best friend, and I find myself feeling that I want to talk to him even though it isn't appropriate." She knew the impulse to be in connection with her ex would continue to arise, so she had to set a boundary with herself that she wouldn't reach out to him—no matter how much she felt the desire to do so.

Gabrielle has a situation with her husband and the father of her children. He has an addiction, which ends up hurting the children at times. "My pattern is to try to control the situation," she says. "I would set boundaries around caretaking him in his addiction, and then I would break them. Now, every time I'm tempted to reach out and take care of him, I send love out into the universe instead—like a balloon—and release it to fly away. It's hard, but I know it's for my highest good and his highest good. Whether or not the love I send out works, it prevents me from breaking my own boundary."

Laura chose a beginner self-boundary that didn't involve another person. Rather than working too hard, she now allows her body to be the barometer of how much time she spends on technology. "As soon as my neck, shoulders, or wrists start to get sore or I feel eye strain, I know I need to stop. I can finish the work at a later time."

Sharon set a self-boundary regarding obsessive thoughts about getting back together with her ex-boyfriend. "When I start to obsess, I meditate to help redirect my thoughts to the present moment." This is an example of a mental boundary around what thoughts we allow to run. This has always been a tough one for me, personally. I remember that Louise Hay once reminded me that I'm the only thinker in my own head, and I have the power to change the channel to a different thought. I realized that my thoughts were like wild horses, and I usually just hopped into the saddle without making a conscious choice to do so.

After Louise reminded me that I have some control if I become aware of my thoughts, I decided to practice letting those horses gallop off without me. I stayed behind, choosing to think a thought that had happier repercussions. This takes practice, of course, but that's largely what self-boundaries are about—making conscious choices from a place of power.

EXERCISE

Prepare to Set Your Beginner Boundaries

In this exercise you're going to set a self-boundary, and then prepare—and set—a beginner boundary that involves someone else. Write down your answers in your journal or the device of your choice.

Part 1: Your Beginner Self-Boundary

1. Using my clients' examples as your guide, decide on a boundary you'd like to set with yourself. It may be related to your behavior with another person, or it may be related to making different choices for yourself.

2. Write down your boundary. For example: *I will not eat after 7 P.M.*, or *I will only give my sister advice if she specifically asks me for it.*

3. Read your boundary every day to remind yourself to uphold it, and possibly post it on your bathroom mirror.

4. Put a reminder in your calendar to come back to this exercise a week from today to evaluate your progress. If you struggle to keep your own boundary, don't beat yourself up about it. Each time you cross it, just redirect your energy back toward the choices you would prefer to make, in order to maintain the boundary. *(Noticing how hard it is to keep your own boundaries will help you have more compassion for other people in your life when they struggle to uphold the boundaries you've set with them.)*

5. If you've chosen a mental boundary—a boundary around which thoughts you will or will not indulge—you may need to have a constant reminder in order to keep your self-boundary. You could use the anchor you chose in Step 7 as a reminder, or you could set a timer on your phone every 60 minutes to remind you to rein in your thoughts and come back to the present. Keep the reminders going as long as necessary to kick the habit.

Part 2: Your Beginner Boundary with Someone Else

1. Revisit your Boundary Pyramid, and look for one to three potential beginner boundaries in the cherry-on-top or good-to-have layers. Narrow the list by deleting any that might have a strong negative impact on your immediate family or work life. Remember that your beginner boundary should stretch you a bit without causing severe anxiety. In other words, you should expect the boundary setting to go fairly smoothly.

2. Choose one of these potential beginner boundaries that you'd like to set, and write it down.

3. Next, revisit the scripts from the last chapter (Step 7), and plan what you will say. Keep the focus primarily on yourself, and avoid ultimatums. For example, you might say, *"Mom, I feel uncomfortable when I come to your house for dinner and you try to convince me to eat meat, even though you know I'm a vegetarian. I'd appreciate it if you would respect my food choices by including something*

on the menu that I can eat. If not, the next time I come over, I'll bring my own food."

4. Practice your script in front of a mirror and/or with a Boundary Buddy.

5. Prepare yourself to reiterate the boundary again and perhaps again. Simply state your company line the same way you did initially—short and direct.

6. Decide when you'll set this boundary with the other person—and then follow through.

Preparing to Set an Intermediate Boundary

Congratulations! You've just graduated from beginner boundary setting. Now we're moving on to an intermediate boundary. This is one that's a bit more challenging to imagine than the previous, but not yet one of the scary bottom-line boundaries in your pyramid.

Even though a lot of my clients' intermediate boundaries turned out to be easier to set than they anticipated, it took work for them to feel ready to set them. Most of us go through a pretty intense period as we're learning to set progressively more emotionally charged boundaries.

If you find yourself feeling afraid as you think of an intermediate boundary in your own life, remember that you can—and must—proceed at the pace that feels right for you. Make sure you're working toward the boundary every day, even if that just means meditating on it, journaling about it, and talking with trusted friends. This way you guard against stalling forever; there's a fine line between rushing yourself and avoiding progress. But you are the only one who can give yourself permission to set this boundary, and you're the only one who will know when the time is right.

If there's an intermediate boundary you'd like to put into place but aren't yet willing or ready, it can be very helpful to openly admit that to yourself. Name what's true, and forgive yourself for being human. At least right now, you have chosen *not* to set that boundary—and that's okay. The steps in this book are designed to prime you so that *eventually*, you'll have the courage to set all of the boundaries on your pyramid. That may happen next month, next year, or five years down the line. Everyone gets to proceed at their own pace.

At the same time, it's true that boundary setting sometimes requires that you take a deep breath and bravely jump in. Courage is strengthened through action, and it locks and loads once you verbalize the boundary. Each time you set a boundary and survive, your courage increases.

Remember, too, that you can always revise your boundaries. You may have to test some of them first to see if they're just right. Let's say you told your mother that you will no longer answer calls after 9 P.M. As a result, she starts calling you more during the daytime hours, trying in her own way to honor your boundary. But the calls are still too much for your comfort because they interfere with what you need to get done. You may have to tell her that you'll only answer her calls when you're available to talk. Then, you'll have to be unwavering and allow some of her calls to go to voice mail. She may not alter her behavior, so you'll have to set and keep your own limits in order to protect your time (and sanity).

The most important shift to make is to set your boundary *consciously* rather than reverting to autopilot—allowing your boundaries to be crossed out of habit, because it's familiar. Watch for any covert avoidance tactics. What do you say in your mind to talk yourself out of setting a boundary that you know would be good for you? Are you scaring yourself with the "what ifs" and worst-case scenarios? Once you become aware of your own tricks, you can stop them before they start. The goal is to learn to make choices from a conscious and rational place, rather than letting your mind take your emotions on a frightening ride.

Before you actually set your intermediate boundary, let's discuss some of the issues that might come up.

Living with the Consequences of *Not* Setting a Boundary

What if setting one of your boundaries would result in unintended—and untenable—consequences? Let's say your father is 85 years old, and he's always been somewhat mentally ill. He's demanding and difficult, and it's hard to be around him at times. You might have tried to set boundaries with him in the past, such as, "Dad, if you continue to tell me what an awful person I am, I'm not going to visit you anymore." But what if he doesn't stop? Are you really going to stop visiting your elderly father? Maybe, maybe not.

The reality of the situation is probably that your father isn't going to alter his behavior at this point in his life. You may even feel compassion for his unhealed childhood trauma and his inability to change at this age. You could choose to erase him from your life, but you may also decide to live with the unpleasantness in order to spend time with him in his last days. In that case, consider setting a self-boundary, if possible: promise yourself that you'll walk out of the room when he's being mean and come back later.

It pains me how many people stay in abusive situations out of the fear of being alone, the fear of hurting someone else, or the fear of conflict. But regardless, the decision is yours alone to make. After all, it's your life. You can choose to set a boundary if a situation or relationship is causing you harm or diminishing your joy, or you can choose to live with the consequences (and benefits) of not setting the boundary—like staying connected to a parent even when they're difficult.

Realizing that the choice is yours keeps the toxicity of victim mind-set at bay. You may still feel frustrated and resentful about the situation, but you can't blame the other person for those feelings anymore. You've acknowledged that it's *your* decision whether to stay in situations in which you've previously felt trapped, caught, or out of control. You have much more agency than you've realized or given yourself credit for.

So whatever choice you make, do it from a place of empowerment, acknowledging that you are in the driver's seat. If not setting a boundary works best for you, there's no shame in that. Just know that any discomfort you experience from that point onward is your own responsibility, nobody else's.

Make Peace with the Consequences

While I've just given you permission to *not* set certain boundaries, I'm simultaneously working you toward setting an intermediate boundary that you *are* ready to set.

That said, every boundary has *some* consequences. Before you set this boundary, it's helpful to acknowledge and make peace with the consequences that might result. For most boundaries you plan to set, I suggest going through the exercise of writing your three lists: (1) the Dreaded List of Consequences/worst-case scenarios, (2) the consequences if you *don't* set the boundary, and (3) the benefits of setting the boundary. (This is an especially helpful exercise if you're struggling to decide whether or not you want to take the risk.)

Before you verbalize the boundary to the other person, sit with what you anticipate will happen, and say okay to the possible consequences. Read through the other lists to gather your courage and remind yourself why you're taking the risk. For example, my client Ivy had a situation with a neighbor who liked to smoke in the hallway of their apartment building. The smoke would waft under her door and cause her to cough in her own apartment. She put up with it for a long time before she finally decided to ask her neighbor to stop. She knew he was cranky, so she had to make peace with the possible consequences of confronting him. She imagined he might bear a grudge, call her rude names, spread negative rumors about her, or make living in the building harder for her. She weighed the benefits and potential costs, and decided she had to set the boundary. In preparation, she wrote her script. It said, "I don't know if you realize it, but when you smoke, it comes into my apartment and causes me to cough. I'd appreciate it if you wouldn't smoke in the hallway."

Her neighbor reacted exactly as Ivy feared. He was belligerent and said, "I have a right to smoke in the hallway, so too bad."

Since Ivy had prepared herself for this possibility, she was ready with the remainder of her script. "Actually, you don't have a right to smoke in the hallway because it's against the law in this state to smoke in public areas. If you continue to smoke here, I'll have to report you to the landlord."

Her neighbor called her a name and walked back into his apartment in a huff. Whenever he runs into Ivy, he's cold and unfriendly. *But he hasn't smoked in the hallway since.* As far as she's concerned, his hostility is a small price to pay for clean air in her own apartment and hallway. While setting the boundary was unpleasant, she has no regrets.

"When my friend doesn't get her way, she gets upset," Sharon says. "In the past, our relationship has always had an eventual blowup and breakup. Then time goes by, and we make up, followed by another blowup. I love her, and I realize that part of the reason we have the blowups is that I don't set boundaries for fear of disappointing her. But the resentment builds up until I get angry, which in turn makes *her* angry. I do enjoy our friendship, and we're currently in the process of reconnecting. This time, though, I'm more aware of the boundaries I need to set with her. Things have been going better for us now that I'm clear on what I want and need, and I've stopped sugarcoating out of the fear of her reaction. Sometimes she gets upset, but she doesn't stay that way very long because I explain to her that it's just what I need."

Do any of these examples of intermediate boundaries resonate for you? I hope so. Because now is the time: in the exercise that follows, you're going to choose—and set—an intermediate boundary that will transform some corner of *your* life for the better.

EXERCISE

Choose Your Intermediate Boundary

In this exercise, you'll decide on the intermediate boundary you want to set. This is a good-to-have boundary that is a bit more challenging than the one you set earlier in this step, but not one of the most difficult boundaries for you. Write down your answers to the exercise steps in a journal or on the device of your choice.

1. Revisit your Boundary Pyramid, and review it for intermediate boundaries. You'll know it's an intermediate-level boundary because it feels like a boundary that's neither very easy nor very hard. Most of my clients end up choosing this boundary from the good-to-have layer of their pyramid. Feel free to choose a brand-new boundary that wasn't previously on your pyramid if the examples in this chapter brought a new one to mind.

2. With this boundary in mind, write your Dreaded List of Consequences. What do you fear might happen if you set this boundary? What is the worst-case scenario? Is there anything you might lose that you value? How might this boundary negatively impact people you love and care about?

3. Now, in a separate list, write down the consequences you have already suffered as a result of not setting this boundary, as well as the consequences you're likely to suffer in the future if you allow this situation to continue unchanged.

4. Make a third list, this time noting the benefits you will enjoy if you set this boundary. What positive outcomes are you hoping for? What will life feel like once this boundary is set and everyone you love is still fine?

5. It's time to write your script, along with your company line. In most cases, intermediate boundaries involve another person. If so, you'll want to make a request first (Plan A)—checking in to see if the other person is willing to respect the boundary you're requesting. Remember to focus the request on how you feel, rather than applying blame. *For example, "I feel uncomfortable when you have more than two drinks. Would you be willing to have only two drinks from now on when we go out together?"* Notice how this example focuses primarily on how *you* feel, rather than being accusatory. If the individual refuses or does not state a clear yes, you might move on to Plan B/your company line, saying, *"The next time you have more than two drinks, I will call an Uber and head home on my own."* Then, start preparing yourself mentally to follow through—imagine yourself walking out of the restaurant or bar, opening the Uber app, and riding home by yourself.

6. Practice your script repeatedly in the mirror until you have it memorized. It's best to practice with a Boundary Buddy as well, if possible.

7. Choose a specific date and time when you will set your boundary, and then do it!

I want to take a moment to congratulate you for making it this far. Your bravery is epic! Most people live in fear of setting boundaries their whole lives. Not you, my badass friend! You've built the muscle, and you're ready for the final challenge. Yes, it's time to pick one of your more difficult, bottom-line boundaries—and imagine how life will improve once it's in place. I know it can be scary, but I also know you can do it. Remember, I'll be here beside you the whole way!

REMEMBER

Practice makes awesome!

SET YOUR BOTTOM-LINE BOUNDARY

Valerie's bottom-line boundary has been a long time coming. She and her ex split up a few years ago, but they are still living together. He continues to be verbally abusive to her, constantly putting her down, telling her she's stupid and worthless. She walks on eggshells around him because he's so easily triggered that just buying what he deems to be the wrong kind of cereal can set him off into a rage.

She wants to move out, but she has struggled financially to find viable alternative housing. Recently, she has come to terms with her own emotional attachment to her ex-husband. A part of her doesn't want to leave him in spite of his abuse.

Nevertheless, she has set a bottom-line boundary that she will walk away from all abusive situations in her life. At the same time, she has begun her search for alternative housing. In the meantime, in order to maintain her boundary, she has had to find another place to go when he becomes abusive.

Valerie's stomach turns when she thinks of her Dreaded List of Consequences for setting her bottom-line boundary. "I will upset my ex and anyone I need to rely on to house me the nights he becomes abusive. I will invite their anger and negative reactions. I won't be liked. I will be called names. I will be lectured. I'll invite more abuse. And my worst fear—I'll end up homeless."

But she also feels sick imagining what will transpire if she *doesn't* set the boundary. She's still vulnerable to her ex-husband's criticism and accusations, and the long-term abuse has taken a terrible toll on her. It's easy for her to begin beating up on herself emotionally, especially after an abusive episode with him, so she is constantly depressed. She knows that not setting her boundary will further erode her sense of self. "I can't let that happen since I'm now rebuilding what was torn down," she says. "There's no other option but setting this boundary."

She's between the proverbial rock and hard place, which is often where my clients need to arrive before they're ready to draw the line. Facing what feels like two scary and upsetting options—to set the boundary or not to set the boundary—they have to choose the one that points toward a better future on the other side.

That's exactly the difficult step Valerie has to take. (As of this writing, she is still working toward the ultimate boundary of moving out and finding her own place to live.)

In her List of Exhilarating Outcomes, she imagined what her life will be like when she finally sets her most important boundaries: "I'll be free to be me. I will feel the power surging within me. I'll feel support from spirit and perhaps from other new people. I will be stronger. I will honor myself for this boundary and move forward in a powerful way in my life."

In order to prepare herself for setting the boundary, she used the playbook script from Step 7 to anticipate what her ex might say: "If he says or does _____, then I will say or do _____." Valerie wrote: "If my ex argues with me and contradicts what I'm saying, feeling, or thinking, I'll say, 'I'm not willing to continue this conversation,' and walk away. If he comes after me, yelling his arguments, I'll keep moving and go somewhere else. If he keeps bugging me and tries to change my mind upon my return, I will tell him, 'I'm not available for this conversation,' and I'll call a friend and ask to spend the night at her place."

Elaine, too, reached her limit recently. Her college student son and his friends were passing through town one night and needed a place to stay. She opened her home to them and invited them to have dinner with the family. "My son and his friends arrived and then went to the local brewery. I had given him a credit card attached to my account a long time ago, and I told him he could use it to pick up Chinese food for all of us on his way home," she explains. "When I called him at 8:00 to see where they were, he said they weren't ready to leave and that the rest of the family should eat by ourselves. I was slightly annoyed, but I set about deciding what we would have for dinner. A little while later, my son texted me, asking if it was okay to use my credit card to buy all of his friends dinner from a food truck, rather than bringing food home. It wasn't okay with me. When they were going to eat at my house, I felt like it was my obligation to make or order the meal. When the plans changed, I didn't feel that I had to pay for their food. But rather than stating my boundary, I simply didn't answer his text. My son ended up paying for everyone's dinner with my credit card in spite of the fact that it was exactly what

I didn't want. It was typical of me to allow my son to cross my boundary in this way, especially with regard to finances, so as far as he was concerned, it was just a normal situation. For me, it was an opportunity missed to set an important boundary I had already been avoiding for a long time."

She readily admits that in the past she has used money to "buy" love from her adult son. But Elaine has hit her limit. She now realizes she needs to set a bottom-line boundary that she will no longer financially support people who are capable of standing on their own. She has put off setting this boundary with her son for a long time because she's afraid he will disconnect from her and stop coming home. But she also doesn't want him to come home just because she's supporting him. She wants him to come home because he wants to see her.

Besides the obvious financial benefits this decision will have for her—her bank account won't be drained any longer—the boundary is better for her son as well. "If I don't set the boundary with him, he won't know or experience how capable he is. He will continue to rely on others to bail him out financially. This was a pattern with his dad," Elaine says.

After she completed the preparations outlined in this chapter, she took a deep breath and finally set the boundary by telling her son that she was canceling his credit card that's attached to her account. "I told him I have full confidence in him to be able to support himself at age 24," she says. "I asked him to be direct if there's something he needs from me, and I'll be honest with him if I can provide it." Her son seemed to handle the news well, but Elaine knows it will take strength on her part to maintain this boundary.

In both Elaine's and Valerie's cases, setting the bottom-line boundary felt terrifying. Valerie's fear of losing housing and Elaine's fear of losing her son were real, and those fears had kept them both in painful situations for a long time before they were ready to set their boundaries.

In this second-to-last step, you'll work through a three-part process to prepare yourself for setting your own bottom-line boundary. As you imagine taking this next step, you might be feeling a shudder of terror as Elaine and Valerie felt. If so, you are not alone. But if you've done the exercises so far in this book, I promise you are also ready.

Compromise and Collaboration

Before you work on the three-part process for setting your bottom-line boundary, let's talk briefly about negotiation, compromise, and collaboration with regard to boundaries.

Some of our boundaries are absolutely nonnegotiable. In Valerie's case, for example, there's no negotiating or compromising the acceptance of any abuse whatsoever. But there are times when you will want to strike a balance between acquiescing out of fear (the codependent way) and digging your heels in at any cost. You need to be sure that you can live with the terms of your boundary.

Laura's bottom-line boundary was set with her mother. "I used to accompany my mom on long drives to visit my brother and his family for Thanksgiving. My brother drinks heavily every day, and on those trips he would become very disrespectful to both of us," she says. "A few years ago, he was so rude that I vowed not to go with my mother ever again. But the next year, I caved. It wasn't about my brother; I just felt too sorry for my mother. This year, though, I realized if she wants to stay in this dysfunctional relationship with my brother, that's her choice. So we negotiated with each other. I agreed to take the trip with her, but insisted we stay at a hotel rather than at my brother's house. His kids came over to see us, and we visited with other relatives. We only stopped by his house long enough to drop off his kids and say a quick goodbye before we left. My mother has asked me to visit my brother with her again, but I tell her the only way I'll go with her is if we stick to our prior arrangement and stay at a hotel. I won't participate in condoning his behavior or enabling other family members in pretending there isn't a problem. I can't live with myself if I lose self-respect. It's too high a cost to me."

For a long time, I had a nonnegotiable bottom-line boundary about working at home. When Aaron and I moved to a new house, however, he had a nonnegotiable bottom-line boundary about both of us *not* working at home. He wanted home to be a separate space from our working lives. So how did we deal with this conflict? We were at a stalemate, and the conflict about the situation was unsustainable. One of us had to make a choice, so I chose to negotiate. We collaborated on a plan to share an office outside the home. I was absolutely resistant to this at first, but I came to love the arrangement. The office was only two blocks away from our house, and it allowed me to easily switch gears between home time and work time.

I realized that for a long time, I'd been digging in my heels on the work-at-home issue out of habit and fear. But I discovered that sometimes it makes sense to be flexible and make different choices—if the new choice will serve us better or make another desire possible. In this case, thinking twice about my boundary allowed me to honor the connection between Aaron and me, as well as approach our working situation in a collaborative way. Out of that collaboration, I discovered something totally unexpected: I actually *liked* the office arrangement even better than working from home!

Notice that I used the word *collaboration* rather than *compromise*. This is an important distinction. To me, compromise suggests that one or both people have collapsed what they want and need in order to keep the peace. It implies a sacrifice. If there's sacrifice, resentment almost always follows. On the other hand, collaboration signifies to me that both people are "rising." For example, you might say, "This is a 'no' for me, but let's see what could be a 'yes' for both of us." In many situations, you can come to a "both/and" agreement rather than an "either/or." In other words, you can honor yourself *and* honor someone else at the same time.

The important thing to remember is that boundaries, like everything else in life, can change. Flexibility is a useful quality. The problem, of course, is that many of us have spent our lives being *too* flexible, bending ourselves to accommodate everyone else at our own expense. So before you think about collaborating with others, think about what you absolutely will *not* tolerate and commit to honoring those boundaries even while exploring as-yet unexplored options.

EXERCISE

Choose Your Bottom-Line Boundary

In this exercise, you will choose the bottom-line boundary you will set in the three-step process. Write down your answers to the questions in a journal or on a device of your choice.

1. Review your bottom-line boundaries, and choose the one you'd like to set first. Which boundary is most important to you, or which one do you feel most ready to tackle?

2. Reviewing the guidelines from Step 7, write the script and company line you will use to set this boundary. But don't set it yet!

Set Your Bottom-Line Boundary Energetically

On the morning of my divorce mediation, my friend, best-selling author and spiritual teacher Marianne Williamson, was kind enough to call me to see how I was doing. To prepare for the emotional event, she guided me through visualizing the highest version of me and the highest version of my ex-husband coming together for a peaceful resolution. While the mediation was one of the most difficult experiences of my life, and it didn't necessarily turn out as planned, I felt supported by holding the vision throughout the process.

I have heard dozens of stories from people who have used visualizations to create more positive outcomes in potentially negative situations. A friend of mine had an unpleasant experience at the Department of Motor

Vehicles a few years ago, and had to return on a different day to complete the transaction. It was the last place
she wanted to go after what had happened the first time.
So she visualized everyone treating her kindly. When she
arrived at the DMV, it was like an entirely different place
from her first visit. Everyone was indeed kind to her, and
she was in and out quickly. She tried the same strategy
with a doctor's office that had been less than friendly.
After she visualized it as a positive atmosphere, it became
exactly that.

As you may have noticed, I tend to be an action-
oriented coach. I rarely prescribe exercises that work with
the "ethers," so to speak. But there is considerable evidence that the exercise of visualization can have a concrete impact on what happens in the physical world. There
are several studies in which one group visualized high per-
formance while another group did not, and the group that
visualized fared better. Top athletes regularly visualize
themselves performing successfully.

In one of the most well-known studies, conducted
by Australian psychologist Alan Richardson, he divided
basketball players into three groups to test their ability
to make free throws. One group physically practiced 20
minutes per day while the second group only *visualized*
making successful free throws. They didn't practice physically at all. The third group didn't practice or visualize.
The group that visualized improved almost as much as
the group that practiced, while the group that did neither
experienced no improvement at all.

In another study conducted by Brian Clark, professor
of physiology and neuroscience at Ohio University, 29
volunteers' wrists had surgical casts placed on them for
a month. Half of them visualized exercising their wrist

for 11 minutes five days a week. They simply pretended in their mind's eye to flex their muscles. When the casts were removed, the muscles of the visualizing group were two times stronger than the muscles of the group that did not visualize.

My dear friends the late Wayne Dyer and Louise Hay were certainly proponents of visualization. In their books and presentations, they suggested visualizing yourself on the other side of an experience, enjoying the outcome you wanted. With my encouragement, many of my clients have had great success following this advice. My client Renee set a boundary to say no to excessive financial requests from her children. I had her visualize respect and compliance from them in return, and she got just that. "In my visualization, they sensed that I had their best interest at heart and appreciated my willingness to take a stand on their behalf and mine. I'm setting a good example for them and taking care of all of us in the process," she says. The visualization has also given her the strength to say no and trust that it doesn't make her a bad mother or unlovable person.

If you're still skeptical about visualizing, I can understand. Despite an increase in studies, Western culture is still slow to support the idea that nonlocal, nonmaterial change is possible. But here's my question for you: What do you have to lose by trying? Imagining all the ways that setting your boundary can go *right* is certainly more pleasant than imagining all the ways it can go wrong. And we've already covered the latter territory in drawing up our Dreaded List of Consequences. We've exposed the fears we hold inside, and they're out in the open now. But there's nothing to be gained from dwelling on that negative list. On the other hand, dwelling on your List of Exhilarating

Outcomes and imagining it going *better than you would ever have hoped* can help you gather your courage and feel more emotionally ready for setting your boundary.

I'm sure you've already experienced how difficult it is to be successful when you walk into a situation expecting the worst. I'll leave it up to your direct experience whether visualizing your hoped-for outcome helps you, but it certainly can't do any harm. So why don't you give it a try, for research purposes if nothing else?

EXERCISE

Visualize Your Boundary and Set Your Intention

In this meditation, you'll visualize a positive result from setting the bottom-line boundary you chose in the last exercise. Then, you'll create a ritual of your choosing to set your intention for this boundary. For the meditation portion, be sure to turn off all phones so that you can surrender to the process. Wear unrestricting clothes, and sit in a comfortable chair or on a couch. Feel free to play soft music or light candles, if you like. It helps to record your own voice reading the steps so that you don't have to open your eyes, which will disrupt your meditative state. (You may wish to skip the italicized portions of the meditation in your recording.)

Part 1: Meditation on Your Bottom-Line Boundary

1. Close your eyes and take several deep breaths. Relax each part of your body, starting with your feet. Then gradually move up your legs, hips, belly, chest, back, arms, neck, and head until you

feel fully relaxed. *Don't work too hard at this. Just ask your body to relax. As you continue, it will relax more and more.*

2. When you're ready, with your eyes closed, picture or feel yourself on your way to set your bottom-line boundary. You may be driving to meet the other person, opening your front door and watching them walk in, picking up your phone and finding them in your contacts list, or sitting at your computer writing an e-mail. Whatever you're doing, feel your strong internal resolve to set this boundary. *You deserve it, and it's important—because your needs are important.* Feel your confidence that everything will be fine. Be willing to imagine the interaction going better than you think.

3. Now, envision yourself in the act of setting the boundary, using the script you've written. Then, *focusing on the response you most hope to receive*, imagine hearing back from the other person. Make sure you're getting *the best possible response you could ask for*. What might they say? How might they express their total support for your needs and desires? Feel the relief of *not having experienced any conflict as a result of this boundary*. Feel your breathing become slower and steadier now that the boundary has been verbalized, and everything turned out fine. Feel your inner strength and self-love increase as a result of taking such good care of yourself.

4. Now, imagine yourself a month into the future, when the boundary has been maintained

without fanfare. Imagine yourself in a situation with the other person involved. The energy between you is clear, loving, and harmonious. How does it feel to experience your boundary in this way?

5. It's now *two years* into the future, and the boundary has been maintained easily all this time. The unwanted experience that required you to set the boundary is a distant memory; your List of Exhilarating Outcomes is a description of your everyday life. You rarely even think about how it used to be before you set the boundary. Visualize and feel what it's like to be completely settled on this matter. What positive experiences do you regularly enjoy now that this boundary is in place?

6. When you're ready, wiggle your toes, and roll your head to begin to come back to full waking consciousness. Open your eyes when you're ready.

7. You can do this visualization as many times as you want to feel more confident about the boundary you plan to set.

Part 2: Set Your Intention

1. You're now going to set the intention to co-create the reality you just visualized. Start by picking a small ritual you'll use to anchor the intention even more deeply. You may want to light a candle, create a vision board detailing the future you most desire, take a walk in nature, work with crystals, journal about your intention, or pray.

2. Then, set the intention in the following format: Write down your intention, and say it silently to yourself seven times to allow it to anchor fully inside you. For example, your intention might be: "I set my bottom-line boundary with _____ [add name of person] and enjoy freedom and ease, honoring my truth," or "I set my bottom-line boundary with _____ and no longer tolerate the unacceptable." By setting your intention, you are putting yourself and the universe on notice that you're ready to set this boundary.

Handle the Logistics

The next task in the bottom-line boundary process is to handle the logistics of voicing your boundary. When and where will you set it? Are you waiting for a particular moment in time? If so, are you waiting for a truly good reason? *Are you sure?* While I recommend practicing your script several times before you have the boundary-setting conversation, stalling for the exact right moment can be a slippery slope toward not setting the boundary at all.

I also want you to consider *where* you will set the boundary. Will it be in person, on the phone, via e-mail, or via text? Consider all of these options, and decide which will be best for you—and most likely to result in the outcome you want to achieve. If you're concerned that doing it in person could result in an unmanageable argument or even violence, use the phone or written word, by all means.

If you've already completed the other exercises in this book, you'll have your script and company line ready. Learn the script well so that you feel confident you can stick to your convictions, and practice it several times with your Boundary Buddy.

Practicing with someone else is very helpful, especially if you ask your partner to role-play the response you fear the other person might have. This will give you a chance to try out your script in the face of opposition. It might also be helpful to ask your Boundary Buddy to respond in the way you envisioned in the *best-case* scenario meditation. This will help you feel more positive about the potential that you'll get everything you desire.

I know it may sound silly to practice so much, but you're really working to overcome your biology. When the stakes are high, our emotions can become overwhelming—taking us from clear, rational people to . . . well, the opposite. I don't want you to miss your chance to deliver your company line as cleanly as possible. I also want to be sure you have it 100 percent rock-solid memorized, so the other person has no power to throw you off track. (This is especially important if the other person involved has a history of manipulation.) You'll have a much greater chance of success if you know it so well you could recite it backward if you had to. Practice your lines in the shower, in the car on the way to work, and anywhere else you can, as though you were rehearsing your Broadway debut.

If you have practiced for two weeks, however, and you still feel afraid to set your boundary, you may just have to take a deep breath and do it. Don't keep practicing so long that you never do it.

Remember that your Boundary Buddy is there for accountability as well. Ask this person to hold you to your commitment to set the boundary, and be sure to pick the exact date and circumstance you're aiming for. Your buddy doesn't have to be a taskmaster, per se, but the kind of person who won't let you shirk the task at hand for too long. Ask your buddy to watch you for any signs of back-pedaling and to give you loving encouragement toward your goal if and when needed.

Make arrangements to call your buddy 15 minutes before you set your boundary, and again right after with the full report. While you're setting the boundary, your buddy will be on standby, holding your intention for you. Don't underestimate the power of having someone there in the background who loves and cares about you. Even if your buddy doesn't do very much outwardly, the moral support can be the difference between success and never-ending procrastination.

EXERCISE

Revisit Your DLC (Dreaded List of Consequences) and Your LEO (List of Exhilarating Outcomes)

In this exercise, you'll write your Dreaded List of Consequences and List of Exhilarating Outcomes for the bottom-line boundary you've chosen.

1. On a piece of paper, write your Dreaded List of Consequences for this particular boundary in longhand, or type the list on a computer and print it out. You need to have it on paper for this exercise. Write the list quickly; just to get it out. This time, frame each dreaded outcome as a fear, remembering that FEAR is simply "False Evidence Appearing Real." *For example: "I'm afraid he will never want to see me again." "I'm afraid I will lose my job." "I'm afraid my family will call me selfish and cruel."*

2. After you have written every consequence you can think of, run the paper through a shredder, burn it, or rip it into small pieces and throw it away. It isn't the truth, and it isn't the vision of your life as you'd like it to be.

3. Write your List of Exhilarating Outcomes with regard to this particular bottom-line boundary in your journal or on a device. How will your life improve once this boundary is set? This is what awaits you on the other side of the discomfort of setting this boundary!

4. As you read and memorize your script, also read your LEO every day between now and the day you set the boundary. It will give you the courage and energy you need to see it through.

Set Your Boundary . . . and Then Maintain It!

At this point, if you're not a little scared, you may not be working with a true bottom-line boundary. Being scared is natural, normal, and expected. Even with all the preparation you've done, it won't necessarily feel "easy" to set this boundary. Lean on your memorized script, your LEO, and your Boundary Buddy. At the moment you're having the boundary conversation, be sure to use your positive outcome anchor from Step 7.

Once you've set the boundary, regardless of how the conversation went (even if you forgot your script and ended up in an argument), celebrate with your Boundary Buddy. You did it! You may feel your effort was imperfect, but it was progress. Good for you for being brave and taking a massive leap forward. Please give yourself the credit you're due.

After you've given yourself time to celebrate your efforts, come back to the reality that you may have to set your boundary again. And again. In the best-case scenario, the other person accepted the request graciously and will put in the conscious effort to help uphold it. In this case, you may never need to maintain your boundary; you can set it and forget it. Even if the best case doesn't occur and you have to reiterate the boundary again in the future, you are still better off now than you were before you had the conversation. Take heart: you'll never, ever have to set the boundary again for the first time.

Maintaining difficult boundaries can be an ongoing gig, but it's always worth it.

Paula dealt with a tough situation in regards to her ex-husband, Robert, and their eight-year-old son, Paul. Paul stayed with his dad every other weekend. One weekend while he was there, the police showed up in the middle of the night. They were looking to speak with one of Robert's stepsons.

"I let my ex know that Paul couldn't visit him again until I was 100 percent sure his home was safe," Paula says. "This was one of the hardest things I've ever had to do and say regarding my ex. I *wanted* him to see his son and vice versa."

Robert became upset and responded with, "If I can't see my son in my own home, then I don't want to see him at all."

Rather than cave in, Paula maintained her boundary. "I'm sorry you feel that way. If you change your mind, let me know, and we can find a place we mutually agree upon for you to see him."

Two weeks later, her ex-husband called to set up a time at a safe location to see their son. Six months after that, he said, "You're the best mom our son could have. You were right. I had no idea that there was a gun in my home." They cried and hugged each other. By that time, Robert's stepson was in jail, so Paul could resume visiting his dad at home.

Laura's boundary maintenance has been with extended family. Due to ongoing conflicts with her aunt and her aunt's husband, Laura has mostly separated herself from her father's side of their family. "I vowed to myself three years ago that I wouldn't attend functions where I might run into them," she says. "It has taken diligence and undaunted courage, but I'm doing it and loving it. Several times, both my mom and dad have commented about my grandparents' declining health. They tell me that I should go see them while they're still alive, even though they both have dementia and wouldn't know I was there. But I'm not putting myself in a position to be verbally and emotionally attacked by my aunt and her husband for the sake of seeing my grandparents. My parents don't fully understand my reasoning, but they're getting used to my stance. They have both backed off the guilt and manipulation, because it simply hasn't worked. I've stayed strong with my boundary."

Kim set a boundary with her kids, and she readily admits that maintaining it has been a challenge. "My boundary is that I'm no longer willing to accept disrespectful, rude, or mean behavior. This includes the tone they use," she says. "But it's creating all kinds of waves. The boundary itself is subtle, yet I'm getting lots of testing, push-back, and even more attitude than before I set the boundary. I have had to repeat it multiple times. I've had to reframe it. I've had to suppress anger and sadness to keep my own tone in check. I have to stick to what I say, and it has been exhausting. Yesterday, I told my 11-year-old, 'You know exactly what I expect. I'm now going to let you choose. If you want to have a good relationship with me, I'm here. If you're going to be sassy and nasty, I will walk away. It's up to you now.' Then, I walked away. It's stretching and challenging me in many ways as a mother, but I know it's important for me and for my children."

The reality is that you have to be prepared to nurture your boundary for weeks, months, or even years. Every time you have to uphold your boundary, come back to your company line. Remember, this is *your* life. Nobody else has responsibility for it, and nobody else has the right to dictate what's right for you. The exercise that follows will help you with your boundary maintenance.

EXERCISE

Stay True to Yourself Worksheet

This is an exercise to help build the muscle of keeping the boundary you've set. Use paper to write out this one.

1. On a piece of paper, write the company line of your bottom-line boundary at the top.

2. Draw a table with 2 columns across and at least 10 lines down. Put "If they say or do X . . . " at the top of the left-hand column, and "I will say or do Y . . . " at the top of the right-hand column.

If they say or do . . .	I will say or do . . .
If they raise their voice . . .	I will say, "I won't argue with you. I have made my wishes clear. The next time you criticize my appearance, I will leave."
If they say they only have my best interest at heart . . .	I will say, "Your intentions don't matter. The next time you criticize my appearance, I will leave."

3. In the table you create, write down the potential objections you think you might hear from the person in response to your boundary, along with what you will say or do. Review the boundary language guidelines from Step 7, and keep going back to your company line. This will guard against giving up on your boundary.

4. Repeat until you can't think of any more objections/small nudges against your boundary that others might make in the next days, weeks, and months. Use your answers to help you maintain your boundary. No backpedaling!

Hopefully, you've done it—you've set a difficult boundary and survived. If not, you're preparing to do it. Just remember that even if the boundary creates some external conflict, it's resolving *inner* conflict. Congratulations on your courage! In the final step, let's get ready for your new life as a boundary badass!

REMEMBER

Imagine all the ways
that setting your boundary
can go *right*.

REPEAT UNTIL FREE

Zoe has begun to say no to clients more often. In the past, she tried to accommodate people last minute, even when it was inconvenient. Now, she schedules clients when it works for her. To do this, she has to breathe through her fears that they'll be unhappy or decide not to work with her anymore. Plus, she has to guard against overgiving to these clients later as overcompensation for having set her boundary. But incrementally, she is getting better and better and better. Even if it's two steps forward and one step back, she's continuing to make progress toward becoming the boundary badass she is meant to be.

Candace had an opportunity recently to put her new boundary skills into practice when she experienced harassment and bullying attempts in a work situation with someone from a different company. "Instead of letting it go on as I might have done in the past, I drafted a letter to the bully's CEO outlining the facts and saying that I'd no longer be available to work with him. While I'd like to remain conflict-free, that would be crossing a major boundary that I've worked too hard to establish," she says.

Debra had an unexpected outcome from a boundary she set. She has a client who tells her that her prices are too expensive, trying to guilt her into offering a discount. "That's her story, not mine," Debra says. "I'm worth the prices I charge." Immediately after refusing to reduce her rates—risking the loss of the complaining client—she was approached by a company for a paid sponsorship. "They asked my price, and I asked for what I wanted. It was no problem. They immediately said okay." As a result of this, Debra says she values herself more.

Tina was working two separate jobs for the same company and becoming so stressed out that she was ready to quit. She renegotiated a work schedule that allowed her to do both jobs while working one day a week from home. "It was empowering to tell my boss what I needed and how I could make it work, while still meeting their needs and then some," she says.

Elaine has recently set a boundary with her 83-year-old mother. "She craves connection and has a hard time forming close relationships with her peers. I'm the person she wants to be with all the time," Elaine says. "I know she's lonely, so I begrudgingly set aside time for her. Then, we both end up feeling resentful and like victims. She's so worried about being a burden that she's indirect about what she needs. Then, she takes it personally when I don't do what she secretly wanted. So I requested that she ask me directly for the time she wants from me. When she tells me directly what she needs, I no longer worry if she's okay, and I can gently say no when necessary. This change has been completely freeing and has improved our relationship!"

Carla has also become frustrated with her mother's negativity, which leads her to take a victim stance and judge others during their conversations. "Usually, I listen until I get frustrated and snap at her, saying it isn't right for her to judge people. Then, we end up arguing, or I just shut down."

So Carla tried a new tactic, which isn't so much a boundary as a redirect. "I tell her I want to change the subject, and here's a new topic we can talk about." Now, the two of them are able to continue their conversations and remain in good spirits. The first time she tried it, she had the most pleasant visit she's ever had with her mother.

Valerie has noticed that once she sets a boundary the first time, it's easier to set it a second time—and again and again, if needed. "I've been surprised how easily the words roll off my tongue since there's so much clarity on the inside. I know now that I can do something about the nagging feeling of needing to set a boundary. When I do, it feels liberating, even when the result is not what I'm hoping for. The mere fact of speaking my truth is enough to take the next step, which could be setting another boundary or maintaining one I've already set."

Stephanie is also seeing progress in her ability to set boundaries. "The old me would be oblivious to the fact that I was throwing myself under the bus in order to keep the peace or to be what's considered a 'good mom' or 'easygoing' person. The new me is discovering that I can be with the discomfort and defuse my inner critical voice while maintaining my boundaries."

Jessica has made similar discoveries about herself. "I've seen how the persona I created is a 'nice girl' who is nonthreatening. And I've always falsely believed that nice, nonthreatening people don't set boundaries or speak up for themselves. But the sleeping dragon inside of me has definitely awakened, and I'm ready to overhaul my life."

Tina is learning that by taking time for herself, she isn't taking away from anyone else. In fact, the extra time to herself allows her to be more present for others when she's with them—without the resentment she's felt in the past. "My biggest challenge now is to keep checking in with me, carving space for myself even if it means I'm unavailable at times to others who depend on me," she says. "I still have an issue around being a bother, a burden, or taking up someone else's time, but setting a boundary is my truth, my clarity, and my yes to myself."

Learning to set boundaries has created big changes for Paula. "I never thought I'd think boundaries were fun," she says. "But the energy around setting them has shifted from dread to excitement. I have felt so much release."

In my book *Jump . . . and Your Life Will Appear,* the last chapter is called "Say Yes . . . and Then Say It Again . . . and Again." This chapter is more like "Say No . . . and Then Say It Again and Again"! The only way to become a boundary badass—essentially, to take good care of yourself and live a life of your own choosing—is to repeat the process of setting boundaries until you feel free of the issues that have stopped you from setting them in the past. So this final step is simple: *Repeat until free.*

Never Put Off Setting a Boundary Again

My client Bob has noticed that if he sets boundaries immediately instead of putting them off, he saves the time he used to spend anticipating the worst, going over all of the "what ifs" in his head. "I've saved hours of conversations in my head to have just two seconds of conversation with the other person," he says. Plus, anticipating the worst is a good way to build up our fears about setting a boundary.

The truth is that once you know what your boundaries are, you often don't have to "set them" consciously anymore. Your boundaries turn into part of your natural flow; you begin to make choices that automatically keep your boundaries in mind, so a new way of living arranges around them.

How does that happen? Lots of subtle ways. Once you've established certain boundaries and demonstrate that you're going to hold them, the people in your life come to expect them. (Just as they've come to expect your lack of boundaries in the past.) They will take them into account when they make decisions and requests of their own. For example, if you've stopped taking care of everyone else before yourself, those around you will turn elsewhere to get their needs met. When you create limits with your clients, they will become a part of your stated policy. Former clients may have an adjustment period, but new clients won't know the difference. Certain friendships may recede once you set your boundaries, but your needs will be baked into the new relationships that take their place.

When you take actions in perfect alignment with your boundaries, what emerges is a self-honoring life. You will find yourself negotiating with others less frequently, as the choices you make naturally produce the kinds of experiences you *want* rather than those you *don't want*.

This radical shift starts with attention. You can't create a life based on what you want until you *know* what you want! Throughout the process in this book, you've started paying more attention to your needs. This noticing deepens over time, until you become ultrasensitive to your "no"—you can feel it in your body. The slightest suggestion of a boundary crossing shows up as a feeling of discomfort that has become an alarm bell. Rather than numb yourself to the "ugh" or "meh" of your authentic response, you welcome those feelings as your inner compass points you in a different, more satisfying direction.

Not quite "there" yet? No worries. Learning to set boundaries is a practice in progress. Remember, "Practice makes awesome!" Start by noticing when and where you acquiesce to others and what it feels like in your body when you do. If you automatically let someone else choose the movie you'll see, for example, stop yourself and imagine what it will be like to spend two hours of your precious life watching something you don't actually want to see. What does that feel like in your body? If the feeling is a strong "no," consider changing the plans and finding a film you'd both enjoy instead.

Continue to pay attention to your physical sensations—your body is your boundary barometer, after all—whenever you're tempted to settle for what you don't want out of the fear of conflict. Did a cashier overcharge you? Is someone asking you inappropriately personal questions? Is someone at work putting tasks on your desk that aren't part of your job? If you feel your boundary is being crossed, practice speaking up! Also practice paying attention to how often you say yes even though you want to say no. We have to know, see, and locate our "no" in order to freely say our "yes." When we create a healthy boundary by saying no, we say yes to supporting ourselves. We say yes to more freedom.

Find the great boundary setters around you, observe them, and emulate them. In the past, you might have labeled these people as "selfish." Do you see them differently now? Do you understand that they're just taking care of themselves? Pay attention to where you see people *failing* to set good boundaries too. You'll notice that a lot of the conflict and comedy in books, movies, and television shows stem from the unwillingness to set boundaries. How might the people in these stories have handled their situations differently? As you note what they could do to set better boundaries, you'll become better at it yourself.

If you experience resistance to naming your limits, be compassionate with yourself. You've likely spent years yielding to the desires of others and ignoring your own, so it's natural that you'll have a learning curve. When it comes to boundaries, the learning curve often includes feelings of guilt and fear. Remember that if you feel guilty when you set a boundary, it's an indication that you're standing up for yourself in a way that's new to you. It's *good* news! Over time, those feelings of guilt will subside.

A World of Conscious Choice

By now, you get that whether or not you set a boundary, you're making a choice from a conscious place—instead of a numbed-out or fearful place. You truly understand that you're the one who's been crossing your own boundaries all this time, and it's your choice if you continue to cross them.

In order to open up the world of choices that are available to us, we have to interrupt our own long-term patterns that prevent us from seeing options beyond what we've experienced in the past. We have to be willing to bravely step forward, even if we don't know where the next step will take us. And we have to clean up our underlying commitments and avoidance strategies so that we can let go of the bad habits we've relied upon for years. For example, when you're having a relaxed time with another person, the last thing you may want to do is disrupt it and set a boundary. What, open this relationship up to conflict? Right now, on our beach vacation? The truth is that the timing is *never* right to set a boundary, and we do ourselves a disservice by waiting for the "right time."

Gabrielle learned this the hard way. "There was a time my husband pushed me up against the bedroom door, hands around my neck, and told me, 'Do you know how easy I could crush your heart?'" she says. "I took my daughter that night, and we ended up at a friend's house. The next day, I went back. As I think about the many times things like this happened over and over, I feel sad. Before we even got married, I was approached by the school police officer, asking if I was okay. He told me I didn't have to handle it alone. I would have bruises on my upper arms from being punched, and sometimes even on my head. But my husband was good at hitting where the bruises could be covered up, like on the top of my head.

"When he didn't, I would make excuses for him. One time he pushed my head into the door, and I had to go to the hospital to get stitches in my chin. I told everyone I had slipped and hit the coffee table. I was afraid of people finding out. I was embarrassed. I loved his zest for life, but I hated his selfish and dark side. I clung to the good parts and hoped they would outweigh the bad. I made promise after promise that I would stand up for myself, that I would say something, that I would leave. But it was never a good time. Something would always make the 'timing' bad. I spent 30 years setting weak boundaries and not just crossing them, but dissolving them."

Another common bad habit is numbing out from our feelings. This makes it easy for us to override our own boundaries even in very painful situations. It also makes it difficult for us to feel joy or determine what we want. In turn, when we aren't sure what we want, it's harder to set boundaries. For many of us, this becomes a way of being so that we can avoid (1) knowing what we want and (2) setting boundaries in order to get what we want.

Author Glennon Doyle tells a story about how, when she's going through difficult feelings, she first goes shopping, loads up on carbohydrates, and binge-watches a guilty pleasure TV show like *The Real Housewives* . . . until she reminds herself that she needs to consciously sit with her feelings. We all do this, to greater and lesser degrees, in an attempt to avoid uncomfortable feelings. But allowing our emotions to come out is an important part of self-care, self-love, *and* becoming a boundary badass.

So take a look at your own go-to emotional avoidance tactics. Do you talk to friends, exercise, take a walk, visit social media websites, or play games on your phone? There's nothing wrong with doing any of these things, per se, of course, but once you know your personal brand of avoidance, you can stop yourself sooner and allow your emotions to come to the surface. You can feel them first, all the way though. Be willing to feel sad. (Sometimes it helps to say to yourself, *This is what sadness feels like* or *This is what rage feels like.*) Then you may want to write about these emotions in a journal or a letter you can decide later whether to send. Finally, you may be ready to speak to someone about them, be it a friend, therapist, or spiritual mentor. The more courage you develop to give your feelings their time in the sun, the more courage you'll have to set boundaries as well. You'll be in touch with your truth and able to articulate exactly what you want and need.

When we're in our truth and aware of our desires and needs, we can see the choices available to us and make a conscious decision which choice to make. The more conscious we become of our choices, the freer we are to set appropriate boundaries and create the life we've always wanted. This is truly the heart of living the boundary badass lifestyle.

EXERCISE

Meditation to Revisit Your Vision and Solidify Your Boundary Badassery

In this meditation, you'll revisit your vision from Step 6 of a life as a boundary badass and revise it in whatever way you feel makes sense for you now. Through this process, you'll solidify your intention to achieve boundary badassery.

Be sure to turn off all phones so that you can surrender to the process. Wear unrestricting clothes, and sit in a comfortable chair or couch. Feel free to play soft music or light candles, if you like. It helps to record your own voice reading the steps so that you don't have to open your eyes, which will disrupt your meditative state. (You may wish to skip the italicized portions of the meditation in your recording.)

1. Close your eyes and take several deep breaths. Relax each part of your body, starting with your feet. Then gradually move up your legs, hips, belly, chest, back, arms, neck, and head until you feel fully relaxed. *Don't work too hard at this. Just ask your body to relax. As you continue, it will relax more and more.*

2. Imagine it's five years in the future. Picture or feel yourself in the home where you're living. It might be your current home or a new place. Allow

yourself to smell the scents, hear the sounds, and feel the air. You have set every boundary in your pyramid, and there has been no conflict, guilt, or shame related to your boundary setting. You now set boundaries easily and effortlessly in the moment as they come up. What do you feel emotionally? Physically? How has this change in you affected your home life?

3. Imagine yourself at work now. How has your professional life been affected by having set the necessary boundaries and living as a boundary badass? What is different in your life? How do you feel emotionally, physically, mentally, and spiritually?

4. Envision yourself with your extended family. Perhaps you're spending the holidays together. How is this time with them different from the past, now that you're a boundary badass who has set all of the boundaries you've wanted to set?

5. Finally, imagine yourself in a social situation with friends. What's different about this aspect of your life now that you're a boundary badass?

6. Stay in this vision as long as you like. When you're ready, wiggle your toes, and roll your head to begin to come back to full waking consciousness. Then open your eyes.

Watch Your Boundaries Shift and Grow

As we shift and grow in life, our boundaries also shift and grow. After my divorce, I maintained what I believed to be a nonnegotiable bottom-line boundary (a "hard no") against entering into another intimate relationship. Then I met Aaron, and my "hard no" softened into a "yes." So boundaries are fluid. What was true for you a year ago, a month ago, or even yesterday may no longer be true for you in this moment. And that's perfectly okay.

The trick is to stay current with your truth. Letting go of what was true for you before, ask yourself: "What is true for me *today*, and what do I want *now*?" Then, update your agreements with others, as necessary.

The Most Important Points to Remember about Boundaries

This book has been about cultivating the courage to stand up for what is self-honoring and supportive of you. If ever you find yourself questioning the importance of boundaries in a self-honoring life, or if you need to gather your courage to set a boundary that you know you need, revisit this list for some tough love:

- A boundary is a limit that you set to define what you will and will not do, or what you will or will not accept or tolerate from others.

- By not setting boundaries, you abandon your true self. The consequences include squandering this life you've been given by not living it to the fullest.

- You are the one crossing your own boundaries. It's no one else's responsibility to see that your boundaries are not crossed.

- You can't change others or force them to uphold your boundaries.

- You have a choice: the long-term pain of letting your boundaries be crossed versus the short-term discomfort of setting limits and keeping them.

- Healthy selfishness will be a game changer in your life. (See the following section.)

- Conflict can simply be the illumination of differences, and you can maintain relationships even if you agree to disagree.

- Writing and practicing a script for the boundary you want to put into place will help you feel more confident and set you up for a successful result.

- Your "company line" is the line you will repeat every time you need to maintain your boundary.

- Becoming a boundary badass means that you care *at least* as much about your own wants and needs as you do about anyone else's.

A Final Defense of Selfishness

It's so difficult for people to wrap their minds around the possibility that selfishness could ever be healthy or preferable, so it bears repeating. Healthy selfishness is at the core of boundary setting. Until you give yourself permission to take care of your own needs—even if it means someone else may not get their needs met by you—you won't be able to set boundaries.

Many of us, myself included, have held the irrational fear that if we allow ourselves to be the slightest bit selfish, we'll suddenly turn into narcissists. But that isn't going to happen. We see so much unhealthy selfishness in the world that we overcompensate by becoming *selfless* in an unhealthy way. If you're worried about becoming a narcissist, *you aren't a narcissist.* Narcissists do not worry about such things! Plus codependent, people-pleaser types don't spontaneously turn into narcissists. You aren't going to suddenly become something that's utterly against your nature.

Learning to be selfish in a healthy way, on the other hand? It will bring greater balance to your life. As so many people I know have discovered, giving to ourselves first actually encourages us to be *more* generous. We're no longer forcing ourselves to give from a state of depletion and deprivation. When we take care of our own needs first and foremost, we can give from a place of pure generosity rather than obligation or a need to prove our worth.

I know it's hard to believe, but selfishness can actually improve the quality of your relationships. When we remove the resentment that simmers below the surface of unset boundaries, we give our relationships the opportunity to flourish in truthfulness and authenticity.

When we set a boundary with someone else, we aren't necessarily cutting off our connection to that person or creating distance between us. The boundary may actually deepen our connection with them. As we allow for more truth in the relationship, we also allow for greater intimacy. Connection will always be more powerful and satisfying than consensus or agreement.

I've said it before, and I'll say it again: *Abandoning myself for the sake of another is no longer a badge of honor or even an option in my life.* Healthy selfishness is the antidote to self-abandonment. You don't owe anyone self-abandonment, and no one who is deserving of your love will require that you abandon yourself in order to be loved.

There was a time when being called *selfish* would have been like a knife piercing my heart. Today, I'm comfortable with being called selfish because I understand the wisdom of it. I also know that being selfish has allowed me to be generous from a full, authentic heart. I can't recommend healthy selfishness enough, and I urge you to try it on for size.

When you learn to see to it that your boundaries are no longer infringed upon, you open up a whole new world of freedom and possibility not only for yourself, but also for your relationships. It's the only way to become a boundary badass.

My Wish for You

My wish for you is that *boundaries* will no longer be a dirty word. You'll know they're simply the limits you set around what you will and will not do, as well as what you will and will not accept or tolerate from others. And that you'll remember these boundaries are yours to uphold.

My wish for you is to know that in their most potent form, your boundaries will support you to carefully choose and consciously curate what you want to bring in, not just release.

My wish for you is to fully embrace and embody your healthy selfishness so you can become a boundary badass of the highest order.

REMEMBER

Your freedom awaits,
and you're worth it.

ACKNOWLEDGMENTS

Deep bows of gratitude for the limitless love and support of so many.

Louise Hay: For being the beginning. I miss you.

Reid Tracy: For seeing me, believing in me, encouraging me, celebrating me.

Debbie Ford: For entrusting me to carry your legacy forward. I honor you.

Wayne Dyer: For the omnipresent reminder to assume the feeling of the wish fulfilled. And for the briefcase story.

Pat Denzer, Linda Perry, Danita Currie, Tracy Phillips, Reenie Vincent, Fanni Williams, and Michelle Knight: For being my phenomenal team behind the scenes. I couldn't, and wouldn't want to, do what I do without you. I deeply appreciate each one of you, and all you do, so very much.

Julie Stroud: For the depth of your wisdom, insight, vision, and heart.

Melanie Votaw: For the clarity and grace with which you seamlessly bring my heart, message, and voice alive on the page.

My Boundary Badasses: For my courageous clients with whom I first shared the work that has become this book. A zillion thank yous for allowing me to guide you through this process as it was still taking shape, for all the stories and pieces of yourself you shared within these pages, and for the impact each one of you has had on me.

All my coaching clients: For trusting me to guide and witness you and be a catalyst for change.

My Hay House Family: There are far too many of you to name, but I must name with thanks and love: Margarete Nielsen, Michelle Pilley, Mollie Langer, Christa Gabler, Adrian Sandoval, Sally Mason-Swaab, Anne Barthel, Marlene Robinson, Steve Morris, Rocky George, Sharon Al-Shehab, Roger Alapizco.

Gabby Bernstein: For the singular and significant support you've provided as I rise.

Colette Baron-Reid: For recognizing and trusting me.

Melissa Grace: For embracing and loving the fullness of me.

Patty Gift: For your effortless and sacred companionship as we roam around, and stay still, and your devotion to what Lulu left behind. We'll always have Paris . . . and Brooklyn, Boulder, and beyond.

Kelly Notaras: For your unparalleled heart and always getting me because we share a brain. You will forever be my NSLP.

Aaron Thomas: For being by my side in a love that heals.

Mom and Dad: For life and love, which is everything.

Kate Aks: For being the other half of my heartbeat . . . and for sharing Allan, Isabel, and Simon with me.

ABOUT THE AUTHOR

Nancy Levin, best-selling author of *Permission to Put Yourself First, Worthy, Jump . . . and Your Life Will Appear,* and *Writing for My Life,* is a Master Integrative Coach and the creator of several in-depth coaching and training programs, guiding clients to live life on their own terms and make themselves a priority. She was the Event Director at Hay House from 2002 to 2014. Nancy received her MFA in Creative Writing and Poetics from Naropa University in Boulder, Colorado, and she continues to live in the Rocky Mountains.

Website: www.nancylevin.com

Hay House Titles of Related Interest

YOU CAN HEAL YOUR LIFE, the movie,
starring Louise Hay & Friends
(available as an online streaming video)
www.hayhouse.com/louise-movie

THE SHIFT, the movie,
starring Dr. Wayne W. Dyer
(available as an online streaming video)
www.hayhouse.com/the-shift-movie

• • •

GET OVER IT!: Thought Therapy for Healing the Hard Stuff, by
Iyanla Vanzant

*SUPER ATTRACTOR: Methods for Manifesting a Life beyond Your
Wildest Dreams,* by Gabrielle Bernstein

All of the above are available at your local bookstore,
or may be ordered by contacting Hay House (see next page).

• • •

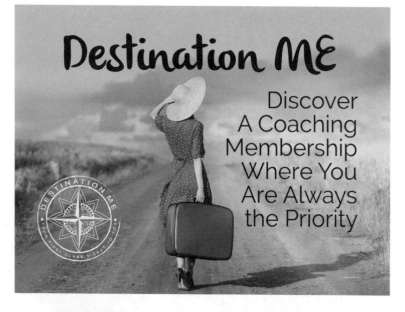

Destination ME

Discover
A Coaching
Membership
Where You
Are Always
the Priority

My private coaching membership is for anyone who is ready to hang up their overachieving, people-pleasing, rescuer cape and find out what it truly means to live life on your own terms! Rediscover and reconnect with yourself while learning how to set the boundaries you need to finally put yourself first.

Destination ME is
Your First Class Ticket to You

Join us
www.nancylevin.com/dme

We hope you enjoyed this Hay House book. If you'd like to receive our online catalog featuring additional information on Hay House books and products, or if you'd like to find out more about the Hay Foundation, please contact:

Hay House, Inc., P.O. Box 5100, Carlsbad, CA 92018-5100
(760) 431-7695 or (800) 654-5126
(760) 431-6948 (fax) or (800) 650-5115 (fax)
www.hayhouse.com® • www.hayfoundation.org

———

Published in Australia by: Hay House Australia Pty. Ltd.,
18/36 Ralph St., Alexandria NSW 2015
Phone: 612-9669-4299 • *Fax:* 612-9669-4144
www.hayhouse.com.au

Published in the United Kingdom by: Hay House UK, Ltd.,
The Sixth Floor, Watson House, 54 Baker Street, London W1U 7BU
Phone: +44 (0)20 3927 7290 • *Fax:* +44 (0)20 3927 7291
www.hayhouse.co.uk

Published in India by: Hay House Publishers India,
Muskaan Complex, Plot No. 3, B-2, Vasant Kunj, New Delhi 110 070
Phone: 91-11-4176-1620 • *Fax:* 91-11-4176-1630
www.hayhouse.co.in

———

Access New Knowledge.
Anytime. Anywhere.

Learn and evolve at your own pace
with the world's leading experts.

www.hayhouseU.com